The IEA Health and Welfare Unit

Choice in Welfare Series No. 20

Underclass: The Crisis Deepens

Charles Murray

14

With Commentaries by

Pete Alcock
Miriam David
Melanie Phillips
Sue Slipman

IEA Health and Welfare Unit
in association with *The Sunday Times*
London 1994

First published September 1994

The IEA Health and Welfare Unit
2 Lord North St
London SW1P 3LB

ISBN 0-255 36355-9

Typeset by the IEA Health and Welfare Unit
in Palatino 11 on 12 point
Printed in Great Britain by
Goron Pro-Print Co. Ltd
Churchill Industrial Estate, Lancing, West Sussex

Contents

Foreword

When *The Sunday Times* brought Charles Murray to Britain in 1989, he described himself as a visitor from a plague area who had come to see whether the disease was spreading. His conclusion was:

> Britain does have an underclass, still largely out of sight and still smaller than the one in the United States. But it is growing rapidly. Within the next decade, it will probably become as large (proportionately) as the United States' underclass. It could easily become larger.

Five years on, how well has Charles Murray's argument fared?

Initially published in *The Sunday Times' Magazine* in November 1989, Dr Murray's essay was re-published by the IEA in early 1990 along with commentaries by three academics and the Labour MP, Frank Field. The academics treated the argument with disdain, contending that Murray's evidence did not support his main thesis. He based his claim on three measures: illegitimacy, violent crime and drop-out from the labour force. The original article was based on data for 1987; the 1994 update is based on figures for 1992.

Between 1987 and 1992 property crime in England and Wales increased by 42 per cent, while America's remained unchanged. By 1992 the risk of being burgled in England and Wales was more than double that in the US. The violent crime rate increased by 40 per cent, so that the rate in England and Wales in 1992 was the same as the United States' in 1985. On illegitimacy Murray's predictions have also been confirmed. In 1987 23 per cent of births in England and Wales occurred outside marriage. In 1992 the figure was 31 per cent. Murray's concern about dropping out of the labour force is not captured by unemployment or economic activity statistics and in his 1994 article Murray does not press home his analysis of labour-force dropout, conceding that other factors may be influential. He concentrates instead on the problem he considers to be the root cause of the rising underclass, the breakdown of the family.

In focusing on the family Charles Murray follows a long line of classical liberals, from Adam Smith onwards, who understood the importance of solid family life in equipping children with the personal skills and moral dispositions fundamental to the free way of life we have enjoyed in the West. In *The Fatal*

Conceit Hayek stresses the importance of religions in protecting the two fundamental pillars of freedom: the family and property. Not all religions have done so, but according to Hayek, the only religious movements to flourish have been those which supported both property and the family.[1]

Adam Smith believed that the law should for the most part prohibit injury rather than lay specific obligations on people, but he thought the family was one of the exceptions: 'The laws of all civilized nations', he says, 'oblige parents to maintain their children, and children to maintain their parents'.[2] He also opposed easy divorce. If it was too easy, he argued, it tended to undermine trust between the couple because both were 'continually in fear of being dismissed by the other party'. He accepted that divorce law could be too strict, but thought it better that the knot was 'too strait' than too loose.[3] And in keeping with his view that family life depends on regular close contact, Adam Smith urged parents not to send their children away to boarding schools because, by living at home, 'Respect for you must always impose a very useful restraint upon their conduct; and respect for them may frequently impose no useless restraint upon your own'.[4]

To add to its value for teachers in schools and universities who wish to present students with both sides of the argument in a single book, Dr Murray's paper is accompanied by four commentaries: one by the distinguished newspaper columnist, Melanie Phillips; a second by the Director of the National Council for One-Parent Families, Sue Slipman; and two by academics, Professor Pete Alcock of Sheffield Hallam University and Professor Miriam David of South Bank University.

Dr David G. Green

Notes

1 Hayek, F.A., *The Fatal Conceit*, London: Routledge, 1988, p. 137.

2 Smith, A., *The Theory of Moral Sentiments*, Indianapolis, Liberty Fund, 1969, p. 159.

3 Smith, A., *Lectures on Jurisprudence*, Indianapolis: Liberty Fund, 1978, p. 160.

4 Smith, *The Theory of Moral Sentiments*, p. 364.

The Authors

Charles Murray is the author of *Losing Ground: American Social Policy 1950-1980*, 1984; *In Pursuit of Happiness and Good Government*, 1988; *The Emerging British Underclass*, 1990; and with Richard Herrnstein, *The Bell Curve: Intelligence and Class Structure in American Life*, 1994. Murray is the Bradley Fellow at the American Enterprise Institute, a public policy research institute in Washington, DC.

Pete Alcock is Professor of Social Policy at Sheffield Hallam University where he is engaged in research and consultancy work on anti-poverty and welfare rights in the University's Centre for Regional Economic and Social Research (CRESR). He has written widely in the field of poverty and social security policy, and his books include: *Poverty and State Support*, Longman, 1987 and *Understanding Poverty*, Macmillan, 1993. He is currently preparing a textbook on social policy for Macmillan.

Miriam David is Professor of Social Sciences at South Bank University, Director of the Social Sciences Research Centre and also Head of Research and Vice Chair of the University's Research Committee. Her books include *Parents, Gender and Educational Reform*, Polity Press, 1993 and with Drs Rosalind Edwards, Mary Hughes and Jane Ribbens, *Mothers and Education: Inside Out?*, Macmillan, 1993. She is also currently the co-editor, with Dr Dulcie Groves, of the *Journal of Social Policy*, published by Cambridge University Press.

Melanie Phillips is a columnist for *The Observer*, where she writes about social affairs and political culture. She moved to *The Observer* in 1993 after working for 16 years for *The Guardian*. She is the author of *Divided House*, a study of women at Westminster, and co-author with Dr John Dawson of *Doctors' Dilemmas*, a primer on medical ethics.

Sue Slipman is the Director of the National Council for One Parent Families, a Council Member of the International Year of the Family, and a member of the Advisory Committee on Women's Issues to the Secretary of State at the Department of Employment. She is also a member of the TEC National Council Advisory Committee on Equal Opportunities and Special Needs.

Underclass:
The Crisis Deepens

Charles Murray

Introduction

Five years ago, *The Sunday Times* brought me to England to ask whether this country was developing an American-style under-class. It looked to me then as if England was replaying the American scenario, and I said so in a long article published first in *The Sunday Times' Magazine* and subsequently in an expanded form in *The Emerging British Underclass*, published by the IEA Health and Welfare Unit. In the autumn of 1993, *The Sunday Times* brought me back to England to see how things had changed since 1989, and the result was a two-part article published in May 1994. Those articles were a condensed version of a longer discussion that is presented here in full.

Symptoms of the British Underclass, 1987 and 1992

When trying to estimate what's happening to the underclass, I focus on three symptoms: crime, illegitimacy, and economic inactivity among working-aged men. Five years ago, I was looking at data for 1987; this year, I am looking at data for 1992.

Crime: When I last visited, the property crime rate in England and Wales (which I will shorten to 'England' from now on) was already slightly higher than America's. Since then English property crime has jumped another 42 per cent, while America's is unchanged. The net result is that property crime is now much more widespread in England than in the United States—for example, the risk of being burgled in England is more than twice that in the United States. The more important marker of an underclass is probably violent crime, indicating as it does a more profound detachment from the standards of a civil society. Five years ago, the public was upset about a violent crime rate that had reached 397 per 100,000 people. That number has gone up 40 per cent since then. Given the reputation of the United States when it comes to violent crime, perhaps this statistic will give you pause: the violent crime rate in England is the same as it was in the United States in 1985. The good news, such as it is, is that murder is still much rarer in England than in America.

Illegitimacy: I will have much more to say on this topic. Briefly, the staggering increases of the preceding decade continued throughout the next five years. In 1987, 23.3 per cent of English births occurred outside marriage; by 1992, the figure had grown to 31.2 per cent. If England continues the trend it has followed since 1980—you passed the 33 per cent mark this year—half of all births will be out of wedlock by 2003.

Impossible? American blacks were at the same figure in 1966 that the English were in 1990—30 per cent. Their illegitimacy ratio did not level off after reaching 30 per cent; it accelerated, passing the 50 per cent mark in just ten more years. The English won't behave like American blacks? It took American blacks 11 years to go from 20 per cent to 30 per cent of births out of wedlock. It took the English only six years to make the same trip.

Economic Inactivity: In the 1981 census, 11.3 per cent of working-aged men (16-64) in the labour force were unemployed, (defined as men available for work), while 9.6 per cent of working-aged men were economically inactive altogether (including those who do not consider themselves available for work).[1] In the 1991 census, unemployment of the working-aged was almost identical (11.0 per cent), but the percentage of working-aged men who were economically inactive had increased by more than a third to 13.3 per cent.[2] It is difficult to know what to make of this without much more information, but the trend is in a worrisome direction.

The other big difference between 1989 and today has nothing to do with statistics, but with the public mood. Five years ago, the idea that England was developing an underclass attracted harsh scepticism. I had failed to make my case with 'scientific evidence', as one academic critic put it. My thesis was not only 'misleading', but 'perhaps wilfully so'.[3] By autumn 1993 when I visited, the idea of an underclass got a more sympathetic hearing. As I talked to people around the country, there still existed an obvious split between the intellectuals and the man in the street, with many intellectuals continuing to dismiss problems of crime and single parenthood as nothing more than a 'moral panic'. But John Redwood's Cardiff speech in July had brought the debate about illegitimacy into the open. The day I arrived in London in September, I turned on the television to

3

find *Panorama* running an unsympathetic portrait of single mothers and the BBC's *Breakfast News* beginning a five-day examination of British crime that, unlike five years ago, did not reflexively assume that the public was getting excited over nothing. Among intellectuals and politicians alike, the larger meanings of crime and illegitimacy were being taken more seriously.

But where does this leave us? An emerging consensus agrees that something resembling an underclass is growing, but there is still no consensus about what ought to be done, nor any clear sense of priorities. People may be openly worrying about problems they didn't use to worry about, but it is hard to find anyone in the Cabinet or the Opposition who has a programme that will plausibly do much to change anything. Crime is bad, of course, but sending people to prison isn't working, is it? The costs of the benefit system are too high, but cutting benefits would drive women and their children into destitution, wouldn't it? And if there aren't any jobs available, then of course nobody can blame men for eventually getting discouraged and dropping out of the labour force.

In this discussion, I will present a radical position. It focuses on recent changes in the English family. The path will be long and winding, but it comes down to three themes:

First, the transforming nature of the change in the English family has to be faced squarely. Too much of the debate still proceeds from a foggy impression that people have always been complaining about the breakdown of the family, and that the events of the last fifteen years are much like other cycles in English history that England has survived nicely. We may debate endlessly about what the consequences of the changes in the family will be, but the changes (which are continuing as I write) have been so vast and so unprecedented that they may soberly be described as revolutionary. That much, I will contend, has to be the common starting point for talking about everything else in the debate over the family.

Second, I want to broach a new way of interpreting trends. In trying to make sense of what is going on with the English family, I talked to many experts from disparate viewpoints, but all of them seemed in broad agreement that the trends pervade English society from top to bottom and that those at the top actually have more to answer for than those at the bottom. I will enter a dissent, arguing that the family in the dominant economic class—call it the upper middle class—is in better shape than most people think, and is likely to get better. Meanwhile, deterioration is likely to continue in the lower classes. My thesis is that English society is likely to break into a new class system, drastically unlike the old and much more hostile to free institutions.

Third, I want to prompt consideration of a new range of responses. The policy options that are currently under consideration in England seem almost perversely irrelevant to the nature of the problem. I will contend that solutions are not going to be found in minor fiddling with the benefit system. A top-to-bottom overhaul of the benefit system is necessary, and it must start with answers to an elemental question: What is it worth to restore the two-parent family as the norm throughout English society?

To begin, I will lay some groundwork on four basics about the family: illegitimacy, divorce, cohabitation, and their current relationship to social class. None of the material is particularly controversial—most of the numbers come straight from the census, and are straightforward—but perspective is vital if one is to see how authentically revolutionary the changes have been. Then, I will turn to the likely effects of the revolution on English society. Finally comes the question of what, if anything, can be done.

The Statistical State of the British Family

Illegitimacy

The basics about illegitimacy are available for England as few other countries, going all the way back to the last years of Henry VIII. Figure 1 (p. 33) shows the percentage of children born outside of marriage (in five-year averages) first based on parish ecclesiastical records and, since the 1840s, on the civil register.

As Henry VIII was ending his reign, the ecclesiastical records of the time recorded 4.4 per cent of births to single women.

5

When Elizabeth II took the throne 500 years later, an almost identical 4.8 per cent of births were to single women. In between, the percentage dipped to its all-time low under Cromwell (no surprise there) and hits its all-time high at the end of World War II (no surprise there either), and otherwise moved within a very narrow range. Up until the middle of this century, about 95 per cent of English and Welsh children had been born to married parents for at least 500 years, give or take a few percentage points.

The numbers began moving up in the last half of the 1950s and continued to climb during the 1960s and first half of the 1970s—rapidly by Britain's historic standards, but still amounting to only a few tenths of a percentage point per year. As late as 1976, only 9.2 per cent of English children were born out of wedlock. Then, for reasons we will consider subsequently, illegitimacy in England exploded. The trendline tilted sharply upward in 1977-80, and accelerated again the early 1980s. In the last few years, the rate of increase has slackened, but only fractionally.

Even if the illegitimacy were to stop right where it is (which it won't), the extent of the change has been phenomenal. It is easy to become inured to numbers, so perhaps this is a good time to pause for a moment to contemplate that figure of 31.2 per cent. Almost one of every three children born to English parents is being born outside of marriage. You do not have to be a traditionalist to acknowledge that this is an astonishing development.

Falling Marriage, Booming Divorce

In the complicated world of causation in the social statistics, the story for divorce is about as simple as it gets. In 1969, the House of Commons passed the Divorce Reform Act, replacing the old, strict requirements for divorce with an easily demonstrated state of 'irretrievable breakdown of the marriage'. Divorce became much easier as of 1 January 1971, when the Act went into effect, and the effects of this major change became immediately apparent, see Figure 2, (p. 33).

Divorce petitions doubled in the first year that the Act was in effect, continued to rise, then more or less stabilised in the late 1970s at an annual rate, after adjusting for population change, of about three times the level preceding the Act.

The figure also shows the line for first marriages—for both parties—which chose the same moment in history to begin to plunge. The two phenomena are not formally connected in any way (the marriage line in the graph is limited to first marriages, thereby excluding the boom in remarriage caused by the increase in divorce). Why should marriages have chosen the same moment in history to drop? Fully exploring the reasons would take us far afield, but a simple answer probably has a lot of truth to it: When divorce becomes much easier, marriage becomes less meaningful, and then less valued.

I chose to use the raw numbers instead of rates-per-1,000 of the population, and to use first marriages rather than all marriages, to make a point. In the life of a community, the marriage of two young people has historically been not only the landmark rite of passage for the two people involved, but also an affirmation of the continuing vitality of the community; a joyous event; a celebration. The day that an impending divorce becomes known has historically been a moment not only of sadness for the two people involved, but an event that spreads a frisson of apprehension among friends and neighbours. A divorce is a sign of things falling apart; an event calling for commiseration and much concerned whispering. As recently as the late 1960s, England was a place where the events of vitality and celebration outnumbered the events of things-falling-apart and sadness by six to one. As of the early 1990s, they were about evenly split.

Cohabitation

This brings us to a more benign way of looking at changes in the family. Joint registration of children born out of wedlock has risen. Cohabitation has risen. Often, people marry after cohabiting. Taken together, these trends should quiet at least some of the alarm about the rise in illegitimacy. England doesn't really have rising illegitimacy, by this logic, but rising cohabitation.

Statistics from 1991 show that 74 per cent of births outside marriage were jointly registered. This figure has been rising steadily since the late 1960s, when only about 40 per cent of illegitimate births were jointly registered. Of the births that are jointly registered, about 70 per cent are to parents who show the same address, a proportion that has remained steady for the last decade.

Putting these two figures together, about 55 per cent of all children born out of wedlock have parents living at the same address—cohabiting. Thanks to two recent studies funded by the Joseph Rowntree Foundation, we have a much better sense of what these figures mean. One of those studies, by Susan McRae, tells us about the situation four and a half years after birth: 46 per cent were still cohabiting with someone (not necessarily the same person), 31 per cent were married (not necessarily to the father of the child), and 23 per cent were living alone.[4] In another study of cohabitation by Kathleen Kiernan and Valerie Estaugh, using the General Household Survey, the median duration of cohabitation appears to be somewhere in the vicinity of two years.[5] Only sixteen per cent of the cohabiting women had been living with that person for over five years. For those who would like to think that temporary cohabitation is not really much different from marriages that end in divorce, it is worth noting that the median length of marriages *that end in divorce* is ten years[6]—and most marriages do not end in divorce, even these days.

The Kiernan and Estaugh study also revealed that cohabiting mothers are poorly educated, (43 per cent have no educational qualifications, compared to 25 per cent of married mothers),[7] are two and a half times as likely as married mothers to be living in council housing,[8] almost five times more likely than married mothers to have an unemployed partner, and are somewhat *less* likely than married mothers to be working themselves.[9] Given all this, it may come as a surprise to learn that the average gross weekly income of cohabiting mothers is 86 per cent that of married mothers—£283 compared to £328.[10] The main difference is that cohabiting mothers are almost four times as likely as married mothers to report gross weekly incomes of £100 or less.

In McRae's study, cohabiting women who responded to questionnaire items about how they spend their leisure time, share obligations with their partner, and whether they are happy in life, gave answers that were much the same as the answers

8

of married women. There was only one big difference in McRae's results: among cohabiting mothers who had not married, only 56 per cent would choose the same partner again if they could live their lives over, compared with 78 per cent of married women who had not cohabited before marriage,[11] suggesting a widespread dissatisfaction with the relationships. Unfortunately, none of the data in either study tackled the most problematic issue: what does cohabitation mean for a child? Does the man behave as married fathers behave? How is the psychological development of the child affected, compared to the child of married parents? Here, the research still consists of unfilled blanks.

Combining everything—illegitimacy, divorce, and cohabitation—the upshot is a portrait of the family that worked out this way in the 1991 census: 75 per cent of all English families with dependent children were headed by a married couple, 19 per cent were headed by a lone parent, and 6 per cent were headed by a cohabiting couple. This is a cross-section, based on children who might be anywhere from infants to their late teens, and including children of divorce. For families with children born in 1991, 70 per cent were born to married couples, 16 per cent were born to unmarried couples living at the same address, and 14 per cent were born to a woman living alone.[12]

That is the picture for all of society, which already represents a huge change from earlier decades. But this overall picture looks much different when we introduce the role of social class.

Family Structure and Social Class

There is a natural tendency to assume that changes in family structure are linked with modernity. It makes sense that the pace of modern life, secularisation, and atomised nature of the city would combine to produce more divorces, more illegitimacy, more cohabitation, and fewer marriages.

But the empirical connection is not as clear as intuition says it should be. Take another look at the graph showing illegitimacy from the 1500s up to the present, and focus on the period from 1850-1900. It would be hard to find a time or place in which industrialisation and urbanisation were faster, more sweeping, or more wrenching than in Victorian England. And yet during that same period, illegitimacy went down, not up (crime also dropped, amazingly). The Victorian middle class was superbly efficient at propagating its values throughout society, and its success overcame the naturally disruptive forces of modernisation.

Trying to say that family breakdown is an 'inevitable part of modern life' also runs into problems when it is applied to contemporary England. The 1991 census provided data on the living arrangements of households with dependent children for each of the 403 local authorities in England and Wales. When one tries to match these numbers against the type of local authority, at first the results seem to match expectations. The local authorities in inner London fit the stereotype, showing the country's lowest percentage of married couples in households with dependent children (57 per cent). But in outer London, which is certainly counted as 'urbanised', 75 per cent of such households consist of married couples. The local authorities classified as 'remoter, largely rural' have one of the highest proportions of married couples (81 per cent), consistent with expectations. But marriage is even more prevalent (82 per cent) in the local authorities classified as 'mixed urban-rural'.[13] What lies behind these inconsistent results? Social class.

Since the early part of the century, English sociologists and demographers have used a five-class system to categorize occupations, and referred to them as 'social classes'. Class I consists of persons in the professions, Class II of those in technical and managerial positions, Class III of skilled occupations, Class IV of partly skilled occupations, and Class V of unskilled occupations. Each census reports the number of households in each of the 403 local authorities that fall into each class.

Suppose we take a very simple measure of a local authority's overall 'social class', the percentage of households in Class V, and compare it to the percentage of illegitimate births. Figure 3 (p. 34) shows what the relationship looks like for births in 1991.

You are looking at what is, for the social sciences, an extraordinarily regular relationship, with a correlation of +.70 on a scale of -1 to +1. I have labelled some of the local authorities at the extremes to give you a sense of what the dots mean. The basic statement is that births out of wedlock bear a strong relationship to social class. The lower the social class, the higher the proportion of births out of wedlock. The difference is extremely large. In the ten local authorities with the lowest percentage of households in Class V, 18 per cent of the children were born out of wedlock in 1991. In the ten local authorities with the highest percentage of households in Class V, 40 per cent of the children were born out of wedlock.

The extremes illustrate a more general point. The story that emerges from a more complete statistical analysis is that the England that still retains the two-parent family as the norm is not just the remnants of a by-gone rural, thatched-roof England, but communities that are characterised by high education and affluence. The England in which the family has effectively collapsed does not consist just of blacks, or even the inner-city neighbourhoods of London, Manchester, and Liverpool, but lower-working-class communities everywhere.

You may be wondering whether the same thing happens when we look at social class from the other end of the glass: Do local authorities with the most people in Classes I and II (professionals and managers) have the fewest illegitimate babies? The answer is yes, but the relationship is not as strong. Sidestepping the statistical details, it is somewhat more important that a local authority has few people at the very bottom than that it has many people at the top.

You may also ask whether the picture looks different if I stop focusing on illegitimacy and instead include single parents of all kinds. Perhaps the rich get married more often than the poor, but they split up more often too. But it doesn't work that way. On the contrary, divorce rates are higher among the working-class than among the middle and upper classes.

The New Victorians and the New Rabble

In short, breakdown in the English family is occurring in drastically different ways in different parts of English society. That relationship of social class to family is pregnant with a variety of possibilities for the future, none of them good.

To illustrate what has been happening since the 1970s, I first selected the districts with at least 95 per cent white population in the 1991 census, so that we could focus on the main issues (race is a minor factor in English illegitimacy).[14] I chose the ten districts which had the highest proportion of Class V households in both the 1981 and 1991 censuses. Examples of these districts were Middlesbrough, its neighbour Hartlepool, and Liverpool. Then I chose the ten districts that had the lowest proportion of Class V households. Examples included Wokingham, Surrey Heath, and South Buckinghamshire, bywords for the home of the professionals and executives that constitute what I am calling the 'upper middle class'.

Figure 4 (p. 35) shows the average proportion of children born out of wedlock in each group of districts from 1974 through 1991.

In 1974, just before the illegitimacy ratio had begun its steep climb, the overriding reality about English families was that the two-parent family prevailed everywhere. Even in the twenty districts with the highest percentages of unskilled workers, only 11 per cent of children were born out of wedlock in 1974, and they represented the high end of the range. The lower-class neighbourhoods in Middlesbrough, with many low-skilled workers and the upper-class neighbourhoods of Wokingham, with very few, were worlds apart economically and socially then as now. Besides being much poorer, residents in those neighbourhoods of Middlesbrough also typically ate different food, read different books, studied different courses in school, spoke in different accents, and in a hundred other ways lived lives that were different from lives in the affluent areas of Wokingham. But in both communities, the two-parent family remained standard. The struggling Teessider and the economically secure Wokinghamian used the same social template.

By extension, all sorts of other things were similar about the two types of district as well. Stop and think for a moment about how intimately the institutions of a neighbourhood, including everything from how to get enough people to show up at a local charity drive to the rhythms of business at a pub, are shaped by the structure of the families there. The point for now is not whether they are well or badly shaped; just that they *are* shaped. Life is profoundly different in communities where the building block is the household consisting of a husband and wife and housing areas where large proportions of households consist of adults living singly or together temporarily.

Switch to 1991. Now, there are areas in Middlesbrough (with 45 per cent of its births out of wedlock), and areas of Wokingham (with 15 per cent) that no longer use the same social template, and this may be generalised to the top and bottom of English society. This does not mean that all is well in Wokingham; but Wokingham is a place where society is still organised on the basis of the two-parent family, and Middlesbrough is a place that contains areas where the norms of two-parent family life have already been replaced by something else. In that abstract phrase, 'the norms of family life', lies a complicated bundle of values that can bind a society together when they are shared across social classes, and split it apart when they are not.

Figure 4 uses the only available data, based on district-level totals. Suppose instead that we could draw these lines for individuals in the low-skilled working class and the upper middle class? And suppose that we could extend them to the year 2000? There are two scenarios, one widely held by the journalists, academics, and social welfare officials with whom I talked (and they included some highly astute observers), and another that nonetheless seems to me more probable.

Scenario I begins from the premise that the breakdown of the traditional family is a part of modernisation that cannot be reversed, and that the data for communities and individuals look about the same. Many among the intelligentsia think this is a good thing. The English family is not deteriorating, they cheerfully report, but merely changing. I spoke with others who were less sanguine, but they too were convinced that nothing much can be done about it. If this logic is correct, then illegitimacy will continue to increase in the upper middle class. In fact, the rate of increase should begin to match or surpass that of the lower classes as the old conventions which have held back the upper middle class fade. The future would look something like Scenario I, A Brave New World, (p. 36).

While a gap may continue to separate the upper middle class from the low-skilled working class, it will not be very many

13

years before the norms of family life will once again be shared by people across the social spectrum. In that case, it is safe to predict that English society will be dysfunctional in ways that can now be only dimly imagined, but at least all the social classes will be suffering from the same problems.

An alternative scenario is possible, which looks like Scenario II, The New Victorians and the New Rabble, (p. 36).

The first distinctive feature of Scenario II is that it shows a gap between low-skilled working class and upper-middle-class *individuals* that is already much greater than the gap between lower-class and upper-middle-class *communities*. This is an extrapolation from America, where close analysis has always shown that the relationship between socioeconomic class and illegitimacy becomes much stronger as the focus shifts from communities to the individual. When the illegitimacy ratio goes up in a generally affluent American suburb, it is predominantly caused by daughters of the Class IV and Class V households who live in that otherwise affluent suburb. Specifically: white American women who grow up in Class V households have five times the illegitimacy ratio of women from Class I households.[15]

Based on indirect evidence, a similar relationship seems to hold true in England. Individual-level data reveal that English unmarried mothers are much more poorly educated and have lower incomes than married mothers or unmarried women without children, for example.[16] But I am really interested in the social class of the parents of unmarried mothers. A study conducted in Tayside comes a bit closer to this, showing that the teenage pregnancy rate for girls from the poorest neighbourhoods was six times the rate for teenagers from the more affluent neighbourhoods. The actual ratio of births was even higher, because girls from the poorest areas were less likely to have an abortion.[17]

The gap between English social classes is thus likely to be already larger than the data from the districts show. How much larger? Conservatively applying the American relationships (as I have done in preparing the Scenario II figure), in 1991 English daughters of Class I families were having only about 11 per cent of their children out of wedlock, compared to 45 per cent among daughters of Class V families.

We will probably find out how close this estimate is within a matter of months. Existing English data bases on individuals can address the issue directly, and I am told that studies are in progress. The actual figures will no doubt differ from a direct extrapolation of the American experience, but they are unlikely to overturn the general expectation: the gap between the lower and upper-middle class communities shown in Scenario II is substantially greater at the individual level than at the community level and has been increasing rapidly.

The other distinctive feature of the second scenario is that I show illegitimacy levelling off, and even declining, among the upper middle class. This is why I talk about the 'New Victorians' and the 'New Rabble', meaning that one part of society—the affluent, well-educated part—will edge back towards traditional morality while a large portion of what used to be the British working class goes the way of the American underclass. Given the day-to-day evidence that the upper classes are in a state of moral disarray, this may seem an odd prediction, but there are reasons for it.

The New Victorians

I begin from the premise that the traditional monogamous marriage with children is in reality, on average, in the long run, the most satisfying way to live a human life. Or, as a cynic might put it, marriage with children is the worst way to live a human life except for all the others.

Marriage does not need to be propped up either by governments or propagandists. Left alone, marriage emerges everywhere, in all societies, and evolves toward monogamy. Marriage can, however, be undermined. For the last quarter century, marriage has been under assault from two broad directions. One is cultural, and has been linked (unnecessarily, it will prove in the long run) with feminism. The other is economic—it has become more expensive to raise children within marriage, less expensive to raise children outside it.

For the upper middle class, the effects of the economic assault are difficult to assess. The extremely high marginal tax rates of the 1970s may well have been relevant to calculations of marriage and childbearing, but the incomes of the upper middle class have been above the level where changes in the

15

benefit system itself can reasonably be expected to have changed the attractiveness of marriage. But the cultural assault took its toll. In the 1970s and the 1980s, marriage and its core values—especially involving fidelity and parenthood—were unfashionable and often frankly scorned. One who got married in that era could chalk up few psychic points in his or her internal book-keeping for extramarital temptations resisted and parental duties fulfilled. On the contrary, to resist temptation was more commonly thought to be a sign of a repressed personality and doggedly to fulfil duties toward spouse and children was a sign of someone who was awfully boring.

But the cultural assault was bound to be temporary. It could not sustain itself because much of the assault consisted of sociological marriage-bashing that did not correspond with reality. The proposition that marriage is *typically* coercive, exploitative, and joyless is not true. Yes, there is such a thing as spouse abuse, but, defined in any serious way, it is statistically uncommon. Yes, strict divorce laws used to trap some people in unhappy marriages, but English married life prior to 1971 was not a sea of misery. Yes, marriages have their boring stretches and fidelity sometimes wavers; but people who have known a good marriage wouldn't trade it for anything and many who haven't known a good marriage are conscious of what they are missing. As time goes on, the cultural assault on marriage has receded and will continue to recede, for the most basic of reasons: at bottom, the marriage-bashers got it wrong.

Besides that, sexual restraint is about to make a comeback, at least in some social circles. It may not seem that way as you read this week's lingerie ads in the Sunday papers, but this particular prophecy is not really a tough call. Sexual modes are notorious for swinging like a pendulum, as English history has so often demonstrated so colourfully, and among the safest of bets is that licentiousness will be followed by puritanism.

But I need not rely solely on historical precedent. The natural rebound is getting a powerful generational shove in the 1990s. The birth cohort that came of age in the late 1960s and early 1970s, with its remarkable power to define the *zeitgeist* that it has enjoyed for three decades, began turning 40 in the late 1980s. Lo and behold, the attitudes of its members have been changing accordingly. They are less mesmerised by their careers, more concerned about children and community. Free sexual expression is no longer quite such a big deal. As they reach fifty, which will begin to happen in just a few years, another change will occur, as they suddenly become aware that the end of life is no longer just a theoretical possibility. Questions about the meaning of life and religion that they were quick to dismiss in their thirties will be called up for re-examination. They will rediscover, no doubt with that irritating solipsism that has been the hallmark of their generation, that the deepest, most nourishing ways of thinking about the problems of mortality and spiritual concerns are to be found in some very old texts called the Bible and the *Nichomachean Ethics*.

Some likely consequences of this rediscovery within the upper middle class will be a revival of religion and of the intellectual respectability of concepts such as fidelity, courage, loyalty, self-restraint, moderation, and other admirable human qualities that until lately have barely dared speak their names. These changes will have sweeping effects on the national received wisdom, and on various behaviours. It seems likely that divorce among the upper middle class will fall, for example. The children of the upper middle class will be raised by parents who teach traditional lessons about marriage and parenthood, and those lessons will 'take' among increasing numbers of those children, once again for the most basic of reasons: they are true. And from all this comes my earlier prediction that the illegitimacy ratio among the upper middle class will begin to rise more slowly, then begin to go down.

Is there any evidence that such a phenomenon might already be under way? Using district-level data, no. The rate of increase in illegitimacy among the upper middle class districts as shown in the opening figure has been about the same for the last half-dozen years. Individual data on the social class of the father for jointly-registered illegitimate births also show a steady increase in the proportion of Class I and Class II births that are jointly registered out-of-wedlock instead of legitimate.[18] The notion that illegitimacy among the upper middle class will eventually decrease is a pure prediction, not an extrapolation from existing trends.

This forecast is not limited exclusively to what I have called the upper middle class of professionals and executives.

Presumably the middle class will also share in the New Victorianism, as will the skilled working class. But further down the social ladder, among the low-skill (and low-income) working class, Scenario II assumes that there will be increasing recruitment into the underclass. This brings us to the New Rabble.

The New Rabble

Illegitimacy in the lower classes will continue to rise and, inevitably, life in lower class communities will continue to degenerate—more crime, more widespread drug and alcohol addiction, fewer marriages, more dropout from work, more homelessness, more child neglect, fewer young people pulling themselves out of the slums, more young people tumbling in.

Why do I assume that these bad outcomes have anything to do with the growth in illegitimacy? This was a subject of vigorous debate even before John Redwood threw down the gauntlet in July 1993. The early salvos had been fired by social critics on the right, led by Digby Anderson, and had therefore been widely discounted by social policy intelligentsia as left-over Thatcherism. But then one of the most respected English sociologists and a man of the left, Professor A.H. Halsey, publicly called attention to the dangers of rising illegitimacy. His warnings were followed by a broadside from sociologists Norman Dennis and George Erdos, both ethical socialists. Their 1992 Institute of Economic Affairs treatise *Families Without Fatherhood* provoked in turn outraged responses asserting that it was poverty, not single parenthood, that was really responsible for any problems that children of lone mothers might have.[19] Norman Dennis has since published a follow-up, *Rising Crime and the Dismembered Family*, that expanded his review of the earlier research and was surgically effective in exposing the misuse of the existing research by his opponents.[20]

I was surprised last autumn to find that this battle still has to be fought. Given the studies already available, it seems odd that academics with professional reputations to worry about are still disputing the basic point that, *ceteris paribus*, the two-parent family is a superior environment for the nurturing of children. I understand that ideology plays an important part in this debate, but there is also such a thing as the weight of the data, and this is not a subject on which the direction of the findings is in technical dispute.

Watching the debate from an American vantage point, another obvious fact is that the English returns, damning as they already are, are just beginning to come in. England is in the predicament of Wile E. Coyote, having run off the edge of a cliff at high speed and, for a time, unaware that he is suspended above the abyss. All of the English studies of the effects of single-parenthood are based on children who grew up in the 1960s and 1970s, when the overall number of single-parent children in low-income communities was low. That is, the extant English studies are showing the costs of single-parenthood *in communities where single parenthood is rare*. Those disadvantages are real, but they are nothing compared to the costs that multiply in communities where single parenthood has become common. American scholars have had time to observe those additional consequences, which is why there is no longer an American scholarly debate about whether single parenthood has large social costs.

But these remarks about the technical literature are probably beside the point here, because there is no way to demonstrate the state of knowledge with a few snappy statistics. Those who cling to 'the family is not deteriorating but changing' line would not be persuaded, and those who think the socially destructive effects of illegitimacy are already palpable need no further persuasion. For now, I am addressing the latter group, and asking you to imagine an England in which the New Victorianism has taken hold in the upper middle class, while at the same time the New Rabble is making life in low-skill working class communities ever more chaotic and violent.

A few concrete results seem likely. Physical segregation of the classes will become more extreme. Two-parent working-class families will increasingly leave council housing, and council housing will increasingly be the place where the underclass congregates (a process which is already well-advanced in many cities). This will in turn have effects on local businesses. One of the ways in which England still remains distinctive from the United States is that the most notorious London council estates co-exist within a few blocks of thriving shopping areas. This will gradually end and the American model for the inner-city—rows of boarded-up shops, an exodus of the chain stores, street-corner drug markets—will become more prevalent. As shops and offices are vacated, squatting will become more widespread, and so will fires. See photos of the South Bronx, commonly compared to post-blitz London, for a glimpse of the future.

The people who are able to afford it will move farther from the inner-city to be safe. The rich will tend to seek areas that are not only physically distant from the inner-city, but defensible. In the United States the 'gated community', with its private security force and guardhouse at the restricted entrance, is the cheerless model that will increasingly be adopted in England.

New divisions will open up within the lower half of the socioeconomic distribution. I leave it to those who know the English class system better than I to spell out the possibilities in detail but, at some point along the continuum, a working class, probably skilled, consisting predominantly of two-parent families, will separate itself from a less-skilled, predominantly unmarried working class—politically, socially, geographically. Family structure will be a conscious point of division.

The current debate about crime and punishment will shift. Intellectual rhetoric that decries prisons may continue, but measures that keep convicted criminals in their own geographic communities through house detention, using electronic bracelets and other technological devices, will gain broader acceptance in upper middle class intellectual circles. Outside intellectual circles, the mood will become much more openly punitive and hostile toward criminals.

This bring us to the problem of money. The costs of the benefit system for single parents has already become a hot political issue, but the current controversy is nothing compared to the intense hostility that will develop within the near future. Whatever else you may think about illegitimacy, this much is indisputable: it costs money. As illegitimacy continues to rise, the costs will rise not just linearly, but by multiples, for so many things go together—not just the costs of single-parent benefit for young women and their children, but the costs of coping with young males who are not in the work force and are in the criminal justice system, of children abandoned and neglected, of increased drug addiction.

If the underclass that is to be isolated in this way were to consist of only a small proportion of the population, then the prospect for the country as a whole would not be grim. The New Victorianism I have described is an optimistic forecast for those who share in it, and if the underclass were to remain small, the increased costs, social and budgetary, would not be unbearable. But the English underclass is not going to be small.

In the United States, the downward plunge of the black inner city began in the last half of the 1960s, when the overall illegitimacy ratio among blacks moved past the 25 per cent range and the ratio in lower class communities was upwards of 40 per cent. If those proportions represent something like a 'critical mass' for transforming the social functioning of communities, then the prognosis is grim. England's overall illegitimacy ratio passed the 25 per cent point in 1988. In 1991, 8.5 per cent of the English population lived in districts where the illegitimacy ratio had passed 40 per cent. Within a few years, assuming a straight-line extension of the national trend, a quarter of the English population will live in districts with more than 40 per cent of births out of wedlock. The implication is that we are not talking about a small underclass, but a very large one.

At this point, what has already been speculative becomes too uncertain even to guess at. How will the Labour Party evolve as its old supporters are increasingly divided between a single-parent constituency that constantly presses for more benefits and a two-parent working class that is increasingly willing to distance itself from that constituency? How will the Conservative Party evolve if the social environment shifts toward the New Victorianism I have described? What new political force, neither left nor right but authoritarian and repressive, might emerge?

Whatever the specifics, this conclusion seems appropriate. English society has for centuries been a supreme example of civil society, in two senses: 'civil' in terms of the uncoerced social norms of daily life, and 'civil' in that England was the original home of Western liberty, the country where neither the military nor police in any form were the chief instruments of social order. Under the scenario I have described, English civility in both senses is doomed.

Perverse Policy

Such a gloomy conclusion. And why is it necessary? After all, I am envisioning a renaissance of Victorian values elsewhere in English society. Why shouldn't lower class communities also share in the New Victorianism and see the family start to revive? The answer? Because British social policy, unless radically changed, will systematically sustain the disintegration of the family in low income groups.

A System Designed to Be Exploited

I met the man I will call Scully on an overspill estate on the outskirts of Liverpool—the capital of Britain's black economy— where he helped me navigate some of the rougher council estates. By the end of the day, Scully had decided I was painfully naïve. We ducked into a pub to wait out a rainstorm, and he went about setting me straight.

Scully has two school-age children, both by the same woman. She has £80 a week for herself, £80 a month for the children, plus her housing benefit, and Scully has £88 a fortnight in income support. Then there is the arrangement with his mate who putatively rents a room in the flat that Scully rents, though of course Scully doesn't actually live there. That dodge nets Scully another £100 a month after splitting with his mate. It adds up to £276 in cash for him every month, £400 for his woman, plus free housing. Figure the housing is worth about £200. Then there's the break on the council tax, free school meals and uniforms for the kids, and a variety of other bits and pieces. Total value? Somewhere between £900 and £1,000 per month—referring, of course, to income on which Scully and the woman pay no tax. That isn't his entire income, of course. He has an off-the-books job in Birmingham, where he spends most of each week, returning to the north at weekends to see the family and to register for the dole. Scully's total income puts him far beyond temptation by any job he could hope to get.

22

Scully doesn't worry about getting caught. There are many ways of getting around the system, some of them quite sophisticated. But don't the Social Security people know about the same tricks? Sure, Scully says. But they don't care, as long as you don't rub their nose in it. You have to know when abuse of the system becomes so blatant that the bureaucracy must take notice of it. That's the key, I am told later by a person who has worked in a benefit office. The attitude of the people who run the local benefit offices is that 'as long as it's going to the right people'—the downtrodden working class— these dodges and scams are not so important. Besides which, it's not worth their time to prosecute. What can they recover even if the prosecution is successful? The worst that is likely to happen to Scully is having his income support cancelled.

Does Scully feel any guilt about anything he's doing? 'The system's there to be f***ed', he said. 'You're soft if you don't'. How unusual is Scully? 'I know more people like me than people who are actually working', he answered. I asked him to tell me about his friends who were playing the system straight. After a long pause, he said, 'I'm not making this up. I can't think of anyone'. Another pause. 'One person. My mother.'

No one seems to know whether we can take Scully's account at face value. The Inland Revenue attributes about six to eight per cent of GDP to the black economy, which could amount to about £50 billion.[21] In 1992, Department of Employment inspectors forced 50,000 people to withdraw benefit claims, but such figures do not tell us how common unemployment fraud is. The closest I have found to such a figure involves minicab drivers at Heathrow Airport: of 150 interviewed by inspectors in July 1992, 107—72 per cent—had to withdraw unemployment claims.[22] More systematic studies of fraud are said to be under way. Even this one example suggests that Scully is not too far off the mark.

In any case, I am not trying to draw up an indictment of the Employment Service. My point refers to the reality that faces a young man in today's low-skill working-class neighbourhoods. Does he live in a world where large numbers of his mates are fiddling the system successfully, and where your neighbours and peers no longer consider it a moral black mark against you? If that is the case—and it is hard to believe that anyone is really prepared to argue otherwise—then, judged from the time horizon and the priorities of young adulthood, it is foolish to marry.

The Economics of Illegitimacy

Is the answer to rid the benefit system of fraud and abuse? Not really. The scandal of the current system is not what you get if you cheat, but what you get if you play it straight. I began with Scully's story because it is probably the one that is most realistic. But suppose instead that we imagine a pristine benefit system and utterly honest clients. The story is just about as heavily loaded against marriage as it is for a rogue like Scully. Here are the economic facts of life facing a fictitious pair of honest young people—let's call them Ross and Stacey—who are in their late teens and have been keeping company. The numbers are courtesy of sociologist Patricia Morgan, who is preparing a study of the benefit system to be published by the IEA in late 1994.[23]

Stacey has discovered she is pregnant. She didn't do it on purpose—I am not appealing to the image of the young woman who gets pregnant to get a council flat. Blame it on the sexual revolution, if you wish, or nature having its way as it has with young people forever. Stacey would just as soon not have an abortion, if she can afford to take care of the baby. She and Ross sit down and have a talk.

Ross has a job paying £228 a week (close to the median for manual workers in 1991, and better than most unskilled young men just getting started).[24] After taking into account deductions for income tax, national insurance, rent and community charges, then adding in their family credit and all other pertinent means-tested or universal benefits, Ross and Stacey and the baby will have an after-tax net of about £152.

But suppose they don't get married. Then, they will have £216—£74 in benefit for Stacey and the baby, none of it taxed, plus Ross's after-tax income as a single unmarried person, which amounts to about £142. Their weekly premium for not marrying is £64 a week, £3,328 a year, a 'raise' of 42 per cent over their married income. As Scully might say, Ross and Stacey would have to be soft to get married.

If Ross is unemployed, Stacey has even less incentive to marry, for the most obvious of reasons. Before, at least Ross had a job and prospects for the future. Without a job, Ross has no attractions as a future provider. Even in the present, he is worth less as a husband than as a live-in lover. Adding up the income support for a couple with one infant and the family premium, they would have £94 a week, plus a council flat. But if they *don't* get married, the same benefit package will amount to £108—a difference of £14 a week. Little as it may seem to those for whom such sums are pocket money, it amounts to a raise of 15 per cent over the income they would have if they married.

There are other advantages to claiming income support separately. The benefits of one cannot be reduced to pay off the other's debts as long as they are unmarried. This sounds especially good to Stacey, seeing that Ross is a bit irresponsible in money matters. If Stacey wants to supplement her income after the baby is born, the first £15 of her earnings will be disregarded when computing her benefit—three times the 'disregard' if she is married. All in all, Stacey has no economic reason whatsoever to swallow her doubts about Ross and try to get him to marry her. Staying single makes sense for her. As for Ross, why not remain free? He knows very well he has a wandering eye. He's in the full flood of young male adulthood. *Why get married?*

This is the first reason why the New Victorianism will not percolate down to the New Rabble. In the low-skilled working class, marriage makes no sense. *Of course* a high proportion of young women from low-income neighbourhoods and their boy friends don't get married now. Even higher proportions won't get married in the future, as the illegitimacy ratio in low-income neighbourhoods continues to be pushed by this persistent economic reality.

The Next Generation

This is not the whole story, however. The *local* cultural norms in low-skilled working-class communities are likely to continue to deteriorate, even after the New Victorianism is in full bloom elsewhere—because the next generation will know no other way to think.

When I wrote about the nascent British underclass five years ago, I briefly referred to young males as 'essentially barbarians' who are civilised by marriage. Since then, that image has become all too literal in the American inner city, where male teenage behaviour is often a caricature of the barbarian male: retaliate against anyone who shows you the slightest disrespect ('disses' you). Sleep with and impregnate as many girls as possible. Violence is a sign of strength. To worry about tomorrow is weakness. To die young is glorious. What makes this trend so disturbing is not just that these principles describe behaviour, but that inner-city boys articulate them *as principles*. They are, explicitly, the code by which they live.

This comes as no surprise to observers who for many years have predicted what would become of a generation of fatherless boys. Adolescence and testosterone are a destructive combination, and the only antidote is a civilising process that begins in infancy and is completed by marriage. I am arguing that the civilising process *cannot* occur in communities where the two-parent family is not the norm, and this will turn out to be as true of England as America. The real problem with the 'alternative' of unmarried parenthood is that it offers no ethical alternative for socialising little boys. For males, the ethical code of the two-parent family is the only game in town.

To see what I mean, try to imagine a code of ethics that the unmarried mother can teach to her male children that excludes marriage. She can try to teach him to be honest, not to assault other people, to be self-reliant. But what shall she teach him about his responsibility toward his own children? What can she teach him about his responsibility to the mother of his children? There is no coherent code that both accepts the premise that having children entails a moral commitment by both the father and the mother, and yet manages to sidestep all the ways that a moral commitment must translate into something that looks very like the obligations of marriage.

If unmarried mothers all over England are assiduously teaching their little boys not to do as their fathers did, then perhaps the New Victorianism has a chance of percolating down to lower class communities. Even then there would be problems, because children take a reality check on the lessons they are taught, and reality would be egregiously disparate from the lessons. But it is doubtful that even lip service is being paid to marriage. In 1989, the British Social Attitudes Survey asked respondents whether they agreed with the proposition that 'People who want children ought to get married'. Among those 65 and older, 92 per cent agreed. Among those ages 18-24, only 43 per cent agreed.[25]

If not even an 'ought' links children and marriage, then the foundation for socialising young males is gone. Perhaps, for form's sake, I should not focus so explicitly on males. No doubt there are interesting things to be said about the socialisation of young females when marriage ceases to be a central goal of life. But of all the many controversial issues that have been touched upon in this discussion, these are the questions that most need contemplation: How are males to be socialised if not by an ethic centred on marriage and family? And if they are not socialised, how may we expect the next generation of young English males to behave? In upper middle class communities where marriage never stopped being a norm, and if a traditional ethic revives as I have forecast, the prospects are bright. In lower class communities, where the norm of marriage has already effectively been lost and a generation of boys is growing up socialised by a 'something else' ethic not centred on marriage and family, it seems inconceivable to me that England can expect revival in the upper classes to have much effect. It is not just the economic head wind that will have to be bucked, but a cultural milieu that bears no resemblance to anything that English society has ever known.

What To Do

The debate over single mothers which began forthrightly in July of 1993 and escalated at the subsequent Conservative Conference has since descended into farce as Tory rhetoric about 'family values' ran headlong into spectacularly inapt Tory behaviour, epitomised but by no means limited to the Yeo and Milligan affairs. Even apart from those episodes, it became apparent after the leak of the Social Security White Paper in November that the Conservatives are of several minds about the lone mother problem, and that the ambivalence begins with John Major. Not much is going to happen under the present government except a few tepid reforms, tweaking a benefit level here and re-writing a regulation there, as often as not making single parenthood more attractive, not less (witness the latest proposal to offset child care). Nor is there any reason to believe that a Labour victory would be followed by anything better. On the contrary, unmarried parents are well on their way to becoming Labour's most numerous constituency.

Nonetheless, the present era of political waffling is the right time for people who are not running for election to start debating more radical reforms, because this much is certain: within not many years, a political consensus for radical reform is going to coalesce. One way or another, England, like other Western democracies with soaring illegitimacy ratios, is approaching a time when the economy can no longer sustain generous benefit systems for unmarried mothers without a political revolt. This is the approaching budgetary reality even if you do not accept my forecast of rising hostility between the New Victorians and the New Rabble. Add in that hostility, and the pressures to reduce the costs of the benefit system are going to be explosive.

This means going back to first principles. The current phase of the policy debate need not worry about shaping a bill to be presented in the House of Commons this year, but can focus instead on a vigorous debate about how a civil, free society sustains itself, and the role that the family plays in that process. The purpose of this discussion has been to encourage such a debate.

What shape might the ultimately radical reforms take? A visitor from abroad is least able to make those judgements. Here are a few cautionary notes and general thoughts.

Full Employment

It seemed axiomatic to just about everyone I interviewed that full employment must be part of any solution to the illegitimacy problem. And it makes sense, up to a point. In 1991, the correlation between the male unemployment rate and the illegitimacy ratio in local authorities was a phenomenal +.85 (on a -1 to +1 scale). Furthermore, a highly plausible story links the rise of unemployment and illegitimacy in the late 1970s. Non-marital sexual activity was high in the late 1970s. Girls got pregnant, but their boy friends, newly unemployed, became suddenly less attractive marriage partners. The same thing had happened in 1929, of course, but there was a big difference: in 1979, the benefit system for single mothers offered an alternative to marriage.

The problem is that, even though the combination of high unemployment and a generous benefit system of single mothers might have triggered the rise in illegitimacy, it does not follow that full employment will produce a fall in illegitimacy.

This is not just a logical objection. England conducted a natural experiment in the 1980s. Between the 1981 and 1991 censuses, male unemployment went up in 196 English and Welsh districts, and down in 205 districts. The swings were large, ranging up to 18 percentage points on the male unemployment rate. If full employment were going to restore the two-parent family, there should have been at least some change for the better in the districts where young men were getting jobs. What happened? Illegitimacy increased *more* in districts where the employment of males improved than in districts where it got worse.[26] This is true no matter how the data are sliced, but it is most intriguingly, if depressingly, true of districts where the unemployment was worst in 1981. Throughout England and Wales, 60 districts in 1981 were suffering from more than 15 per cent unemployment among men. In 1991, 47 of those 60 districts had a lower unemployment rate. Their illegitimacy ratios had gone up by an average of 23 percentage points in the intervening ten years, far above the national average of 17 points. This was true even of the districts (such as Corby and Derwentside) where the improvement in employment was dramatically large.

Full employment is a fine goal, and achieving it will surely facilitate marriage. But, based on the experience of the 1980s, there is no reason to suppose that improving the employment picture is by itself going to have any effect on changes in illegitimacy.[27]

The Minimalist Solution: Stop Penalising Marriage

At the very least, stop making the benefit system favour single mothers over married mothers. It is easy enough to do.

Establish income support and family benefit levels such that any married couple receives a benefit at least as large as any benefit that can be obtained outside marriage, given the same number of children and employment situation, under any visible or concealed living arrangements with boyfriend or girlfriend.

Note the proviso, 'visible or concealed'. The financial benefit for married couples must match the *best* financial situation in which an unmarried mother could find herself, which means that married couples with an unemployed husband will end up in a better financial situation than a single mother with no boyfriend. Otherwise, the system retains a clear and present incentive for single women with boyfriends to remain unmarried and represent themselves to the benefit office as women living alone.

This solution is minimalist in both its implementation and effects. It would require only changes in benefit levels, not in the basic machinery of the benefit system. But it is also doubtful whether, by itself, the changes would be decisive. Marriage would no longer be a financially punishing decision, but having a baby out of wedlock would become no more painful.

In terms of budgets, the minimalist solution will be hugely expensive if it is achieved by raising the benefits for married couples instead of lowering the benefits for single parents. I will leave the detailed calculations to the budget experts, but I doubt that England can afford to increase the benefits for married couples enough to eliminate the penalties of marriage if it retains its current benefit levels for single women. This leaves us with the question: What kind of system might be both affordable and restore marriage as the framework for having children?

Facing Up to Hard Choices

A number of strategies *could* work, given the political will. American social critic Mickey Kaus has recently proposed a solution that would replace the entire American welfare system with guaranteed public service jobs at slightly below the prevailing market wage. Many years ago, Milton Friedman proposed replacing the entire welfare system with a negative income tax—a guaranteed income—that would replace all other benefits. I favour eliminating benefits for unmarried women altogether (for potential new entrants, while keeping the Faustian bargain we have made with women already on the system). A strong case can be made that any of these radical changes would produce large reductions in the number of children born to single women. The simplest of all solutions for England that might have a major positive effect? Simply restore the benefit structure (in constant pounds) that you had in 1960.

The time has not yet come to try to make such arguments in detail. Before a debate over any of these alternatives can take place meaningfully (in the United States as in England, I should add), a few hard truths that people have preferred to ignore must be confronted:

The real rewards of marriage are long-term and intangible, but the seductive temptations not to marry for young people are short-term and concrete. In the past, the laws of economics imposed unbearable economic penalties on an unmarried woman with a small child. She was not an economically viable unit. Society backstopped the economic pain with immediate and concrete social penalties. The combination led women to make insistent demands on any man who wanted to sleep with them. Society backstopped those demands by holding out to men one glitteringly attractive and tangible reward: marriage was the only socially acceptable way to have regular sexual access to a woman. It was often the only way, period. Marriage flourished.

It is unlikely, even with the New Victorianism, that extramarital sex will ever subside to the point that the sexual motive for marriage will regain its once sovereign power. But the latent economic penalties of unmarried parenthood are as natural now as ever. The House of Commons does not need to legislate artificial ones. They will occur of their own accord, even in this liberated age, because it remains true now as before that a young single adult human trying to make a living and also to raise a small child is taking on more than one adult human being can easily do. It is a lot easier with two adult human beings sharing the burden. That's the way the world works, until the state intervenes. The state should stop intervening, and let the natural economic penalties occur.

The penalties may occur in the context of a welfare state. It is possible to have a social safety net that protects everyone from cradle to grave, as long as a social contract is accepted.

31

The government will provide protection against the vicissitudes of life as long as you, the individual citizen, take responsibility for the consequences of your own voluntary behaviour. Getting pregnant and bearing a child is, at the present time, voluntary behaviour.

Many will find even this level of restraint on the welfare state unacceptable. But as you cast about for solutions, I suggest that one must inevitably come up against this rock. The welfare of society requires that women actively avoid getting pregnant if they have no husband, and that women once again demand marriage from a man who would have them bear a child. The only way the active avoidance and the demands are going to occur is if childbearing entails economic penalties for a single woman. It is all horribly sexist, I know. It also happens to be true.

Other things happen to be true as well. Babies need fathers. Society needs fathers. The stake for England, as for the United States, is not to be measured in savings in the Social Security budget nor in abstract improvements in the moral climate. The stake is the survival of free institutions and a civil society.

Figure 1
Percentage of Children Born to Unmarried Women 1540-1991

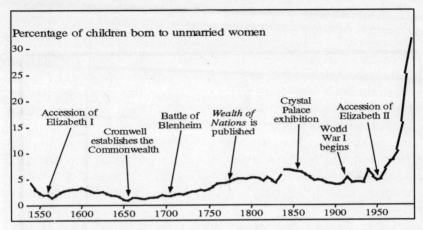

Laslett *et al.*, 1980, Table 1.1, OPCS, *Birth Statistics*, FM1 no. 13, Table 1.1., FM20, Table 1.1.

Figure 2
Divorces, 1961-1991

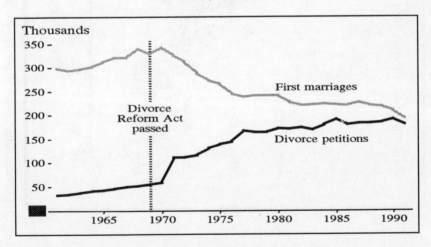

Source: OPCS, *Marriage and Divorce Statistics*, 1993, Table 2.1 and comparable earlier editions. (Marriage refers to first marriages for both bride and groom.)

Figure 3
Children Born out of Wedlock and Social Class, 1991

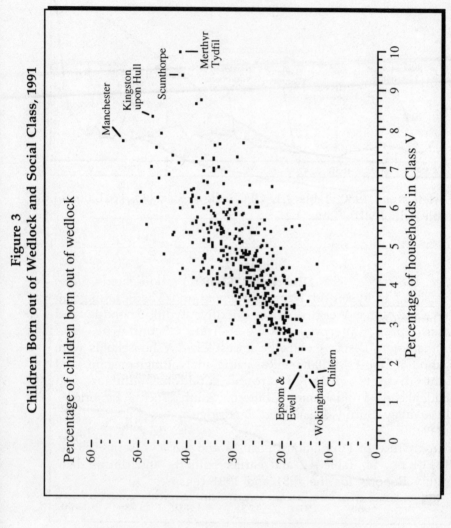

Percentage of children born out of wedlock

Manchester

Kingston upon Hull

Scunthorpe

Merthyr Tydfil

Epsom & Ewell

Wokingham

Chiltern

Percentage of households in Class V

Source: 1991 Census data, County Reports, Table 90, and Office of Population Censuses and Surveys, 1993b, Table 4.2

Figure 4
Illegitimacy Ratio 1974-1991

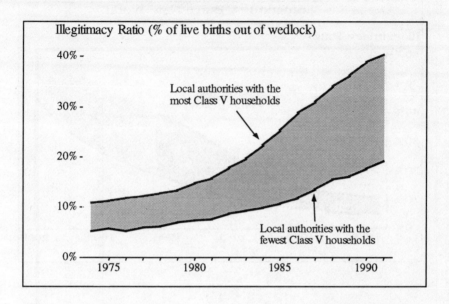

Note: Districts with the most Class V households were Gateshead in Tyne and Wear, Hartlepool and Middlesbrough in Cleveland, three Welsh districts (Merthyr Tydfil, Rhondda, and Afan), plus Liverpool, Stoke-on-Trent, Scunthorpe, and Southampton. Districts with the fewest Class V households were Solihull in West Midlands, Rushcliffe in Nottinghamshire, and eight districts clustered around London: Windsor and Maidenhead, Wokingham, Chiltern, South Bucks, Elmbridge, Mole Valley, Surrey Heath and Tandridge.

Source: Office of Population Censuses and Surveys, series VS no. 18, PP1 no. 14, Table 4.2 and earlier editions, and census data, County Reports for the 1981 and 1991 censuses.

Figure 5

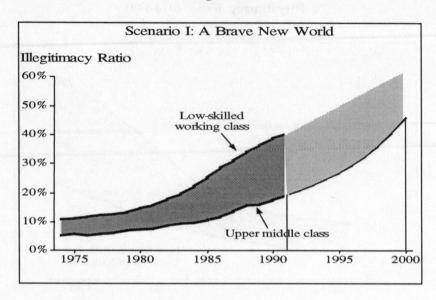

Scenario I: A Brave New World

Illegitimacy Ratio

Low-skilled working class

Upper middle class

60%
50%
40%
30%
20%
10%
0%

1975   1980   1985   1990   1995   2000

Figure 6

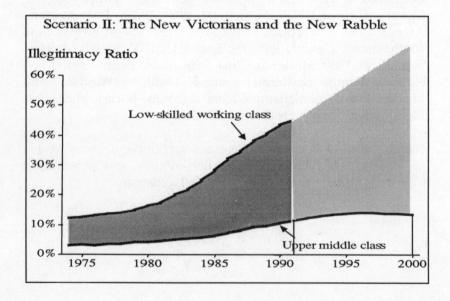

Scenario II: The New Victorians and the New Rabble

Illegitimacy Ratio

Low-skilled working class

Upper middle class

60%
50%
40%
30%
20%
10%
0%

1975   1980   1985   1990   1995   2000

Bibliography

Murray, C., *The Emerging British Underclass*, London: IEA Health and Welfare Unit, 1990.

Central Statistical Office, *Annual Abstract of Statistics 1993*, No. 129 ed., London: HMSO, 1993.

Dennis, N., *Rising Crime and the Dismembered Family: How Conformist Intellectuals have Campaigned Against Common Sense*, Choice in Welfare, No. 18, London: IEA Health and Welfare Unit, 1993.

Dennis, N. and Erdos, G., *Families Without Fatherhood*, Choice in Welfare, No. 12, second edition, London: IEA Health and Welfare Unit, 1993.

Kiernan, K.E. and Estaugh, V., *Cohabitation: Extra-marital Child-bearing and Social Policy*, Family Policy Studies Centre, Occasional Paper 17, 1993.

Laslett, P., Oosterveen, K. and Smith, R.M., (ed), *Bastardy and Its Comparative History*, Cambridge, MA: Harvard University Press, 1980.

McRae, S., *Co-habiting Mothers: Changing Marriage and Mother-hood?*, London: Policy Studies Institute, 1993.

Office of Population Censuses and Surveys, *Key Statistics for Local Authorities*, 1981.

Office of Population Censuses and Surveys, *1991 Birth Statistics: England and Wales*, Series FM2, no. 20, 1993.

Office of Population Censuses and Surveys, *1991 Key Population and Vital Statistics: Local and Health Authority Areas*, Series VS, no. 18, PP1, no. 14, 1993.

Office of Population Censuses and Surveys, *1991 Marriage and Divorce Statistics: England and Wales*, Series FM2, no. 19, 1993.

Smith, T., 'Influence of Socio-economic Factors on Attaining Targets for Reducing Teenage Pregnancies', *British Medical Journal*, no. 6887, 1993.

Notes

1   *Office of Population Censuses and Surveys*, 1981, Table 7.
2   *1991 Census Report for Great Britain (Part I)*, Table 8, pp. 194-195.
3   Walker, A., 'Blaming the Victims', in Murray, C., *The Emerging British Underclass*, Choice in Welfare Series No. 2, London: IEA Health & Welfare Unit, 1990.
4   McRae, S., 1993, Figure 1, p. 20. Of the 38 women of the study who were living alone, six had been married and then divorced in the four-and-a-half year follow-up, representing 4 per cent of all cohabiting mothers in the study.
5   Kiernan and Estaugh, 1993, Table 2.5.
6   OPCS, *1991 Marriage and Divorce Statistics*, 1993, Table 4.3.
7   Kiernan and Estaugh, 1993, Table 2.6.
8   Kiernan and Estaugh, 1993, Table 2.7.
9   Kiernan and Estaugh, 1993, Table 2.10.
10 Kiernan and Estaugh, 1993, Table 2.11.
11 McRae, 1993, Table 6.1, p. 90.
12 OPCS, *1991 Birth Statistics*, 1993, Tables 3.9, 3.10, 5.2.
13 For the classification see for example OPCS, *1991 Key Population and Vital Statistics*, 1993, Appendix 5.
14 The statement that race is a minor factor in English illegitimacy invariably attracts scepticism because it is so widely known that blacks, especially Caribbean blacks, have among the highest illegitimacy ratios. But race does not affect the illegitimacy ratio for England as a whole by more than a percentage point or two. The precise size of the racial effect cannot be computed directly, because the published breakdowns are based on country of birth (thus lumping together white and non-white English subjects born in England). But the decennial census publishes ethnic breakdowns by local authority, enabling at least some probes into the range of possibilities. For England and Wales as a whole 30.2 per cent of births were out of wedlock in 1991. For the subset of local authorities with at least 95 per cent whites, the ratio was 28.7 per cent—and remember that many of the small ethnic minority in those local authorities were not blacks, with high illegitimacy ratios, but South Asians and East Asians, with very low ratios. The notion that the illegitimacy picture in England would look much different if England suddenly became all white is wrong.

15 Author's analysis of the *National Longitudinal Survey of Youth*.

16 Kiernan and Esthaugh 1993, Table 3.5; Central Statistical Office 1993, Table 5.5.

17 Smith, 1993. Older results from the *National Child Development Study* are consistent with this finding.

18 But the trend lines on joint registration are impossible to interpret for my purposes, both because they refer to the father of the new baby, not the social class from which the mother comes (a match which is especially likely to be discrepant where births out of wedlock are concerned), and because joint registration of illegitimate births is more common among the high classes than the lower ones.

19 Dennis and Erdos, 1992.

20 Dennis, 1993.

21 *The Financial Times*, 26 August 1993.

22 *The Daily Telegraph*, 8 November 1993.

23 Morgan, P., *Farewell to the Family: The Rise of the Mother-Child-State Unit*, London: IEA Health and Welfare Unit, forthcoming (1994).

24 In 1991, (the most recent figures), the median before-tax weekly earnings of a full-time male worker in a manual occupation were £235.40. A quarter of all males who worked at manual occupations made £186 or less, *Central Statistical Office*, 1993, Table 6.17.

25 Kiernan and Estaugh, 1993, Table 1.3.

26 The average illegitimacy ratios for the 196 local authorities where male unemployment increased between the 1981 and 1991 censuses rose from 11.1 per cent to 27.0 per cent, an increase of 15.9 percentage points. In the 205 local authorities where male unemployment went down, the change in the illegitimacy ratio was from 10.6 per cent to 28.2 per cent, an increase of 17.6 percentage points. Overall, the correlation between change in unemployment and change in the illegitimacy ratio from 1981-91 was -.19.

27 There are other problems with treating unemployment as a cause: the unemployment rate in 1991 'predicts' illegitimacy in 1974 about as well as it 'predicts' illegitimacy in 1991. Even stranger: the 1991 unemployment figures 'predict' 1974 illegitimacy better than does the 1981 unemployment rate.

Commentaries

Back to the Future: Victorian Values for the 21st Century

Pete Alcock

Getting Worse

On his return to Britain, five years after he came to warn us of the 'bleak message' that the 'underclass' in this country, although not as substantial as in the United States, was growing rapidly, Charles Murray has, perhaps not surprisingly, discovered that in those last five years things have been getting worse. Murray was not invited over to comment that everything was 'hunky dory', and Britain has experienced a major economic recession over that period. Five years later he thus repeats his warnings, but in more apocalyptic terms, and with more pointed moral prescription.

In 1989 the problem was an 'emerging' underclass, now it is a wholesale 'British Revolution'. Last time Murray focused on *three* phenomena (causes?) associated with this—illegitimacy, violent crime and economic inactivity—now he discusses only one: *illegitimacy*. At stake, he argues, 'is the survival of free institutions and a civil society', and what is required is the restoration of the two-parent family, through marriage, as 'the norm throughout English society'. How is it that the complex, and much debated, phenomenon of the underclass (if such there be) can now be distilled into the simple problem of the changing values of matrimony? And why have these changes suddenly, at the end of the twentieth century, reached such apocalyptic proportions?

In asking, and then answering, these questions Murray's arguments become much clearer, and simpler, than they were five years ago. They also become considerably less relevant. The problem with the clearer focus, is that it becomes more obvious what Murray is not talking about. And, as I shall return to later, what he is not talking about is much more important than what he is. Further, his prescriptions for future policy development thus address a much narrower portion of the social fabric. Even if they were both feasible and desirable (which, as I shall argue, they are not), they would not do much to alter many of the pressing social problems which social policy commentators and politicians in Britain (and, I had assumed, Murray himself) are most concerned about.

Whether or not they are characterised as the emergence, or establishment, of a new underclass there is now no doubt there are growing divisions within British society. Inequality is greater than it was two decades ago, and this has accentuated divisions of gender, race and age, as well as class; unemployment has remained at a consistently, and depressingly, high level; homelessness has increased; health inequalities have been widening; crime and fear of crime are rising. And yet at the same time economic performance remains, at best, sluggish; the balance of payments is deeply red; levels of taxation are rising; and government spending is being further pared back. There is no shortage of problems here for economists and social policy-makers; but Murray is concerned only about changing values on marriage and illegitimacy. In social policy terms, at least, I am afraid, such single-mindedness will not serve us well.

To be fair, we know from his previous 'warnings' that Murray's concerns for social policy were quite specifically focused. In his 1990 rejoinder, in particular, he emphasised that he was not concerned with poverty itself, but with the attitudes and responses of poor people. And poverty was not always a problem of attitudes, some poor people, for instance the frail, elderly pensioner with too little money[1] should be given more money—although quite where this money should come from, given Murray's more general concern to remove any role which the state may play in public support, is not clear. Further, he recognised that evidence demonstrated that not all poor people did pass on their 'poor' values to their children. His concern was only that some did—or rather could, we can never know what they have actually done—and that more might.

The focus of Murray's concern then was on moral choices and perverse incentives. The problem of the emerging underclass was that more people were making the wrong moral choices and thus entering this class, and that welfare policies (specifically social security) were creating perverse incentives for them to do just that. In 1994 a new, and more pejorative, terminology is adopted. The underclass who are making the wrong choices are now the 'New Rabble'. And they are distinguished in moral terms from those who are making the right choices, the 'New Victorians'—or rather those who Murray *hopes* will make the right choices. For he admits that his prediction that illegitimacy rates amongst the upper middle class will in the future decrease is pure conjecture. The perverse incentives with which Murray is concerned have thus now been boiled down to the incentive for poor women to have an illegitimate child.

The 'Problem of' Illegitimacy

There was some debate, and disagreement, in 1989, in particular with Brown,[2] about the extent of the problem of growing rates of illegitimacy in Britain, and about the assumptions concerning family forms, and family formation, which could be made from this. Murray addresses some of these problems in 1994. As he points out the statistics show that numbers of illegitimate births have been increasing in the past five years; and he quotes new evidence about the relatively short-lived nature of cohabiting relationships (as opposed to marriages) and tendency for such relationships to be poorer in financial and other terms. This may be true; but this evidence too could be 'sliced-up' in different ways to permit different comparisons. Short-lived or poorer relationships (married or not) could be compared on the bases of class, race, locality or age and patterns would also perhaps be revealed.

Despite the new evidence, however, Murray still does not address the points that most lone parents in Britain remain those separated or divorced (not the young mothers of illegitimate children), that most lone parents subsequently (re)marry, and that most illegitimate children are registered as living with both parents. Of course, changes are going on in family structure in Britain; and, Murray is right, levels of illegitimacy are growing. But as the studies quoted demonstrate these are part of broader demographic and cultural shifts, which reveal changing patterns of parenting but not necessarily a failure of it.

Even if we were to accept, however, that, all other things being equal, two parents are better at bringing up a child than one—and the research evidence quoted does not address this issue—we cannot simply use changing illegitimacy rates as a proxy measure for the absence of a father figure. And, because all those other things in practice of course never are equal, we cannot take either illegitimacy or the absence of a father figure as evidence that a whole range of social disasters and dislocations are being visited upon (or perpetrated by) the inhabitants of those poorer areas where illegitimacy rates are highest.

There will always be argument about what deductions can be made from statistical mapping, particularly when comparisons are made over time—and Murray is projecting back over 450 years here! We need to know whether like is being compared to like, and often it is not. And, as Murray himself concedes, statistical snapshots of populations in 1987 or 1992 cannot reveal evidence of the influence of dynamic social processes, especially those which might only recently have begun to take effect. Thus the evidence, for instance, that illegitimacy rates are higher, and growing more rapidly, in poorer local areas in Britain does not provide proof that the former is the cause of the latter—nor indeed that there is a chain of causation running in the other direction. Much more than a growth in illegitimacy is likely to be going on in these areas, and as social scientists we should know that causes are more complex phenomena than are correlations, whatever the latter may seem to reveal.

To put the same point in more simple terms we should simply consider the following non-contested (I presume) observations. Some lone parents are financially poor, indeed many are. Some live in poor neighbourhoods. Some may be less than perfect parents by one measure or another. Some children whose family was for a time at least comprised of a lone parent may grow up to be unemployed, to commit crime, or to bear or father an illegitimate child. But at the same time, some, arguably many, lone parent families are comprised of devoted parents and well-behaved children; while some two-parent families provide unsupportive or repressive environments for their children. And most of the unemployed, the perpetrators of crime and the cohabiting (or not) parents of illegitimate children have come from what must appear from all the evidence to be stable, married, family relationships. There are other forces at work here too.

Perverse Incentives?

In his discussion of the 'New Rabble' Murray does, however, link the growing levels of illegitimacy to other social problems such as poverty, criminality and unemployment. In particular he argues that lone parents and their children are likely to experience these problems because they become welfare dependents and lose the will to form the kind of married relationships which presumably would protect them from such risks. And lone parents become welfare dependents, not because of economic misfortune, matrimonial breakdown or exclusion from the labour market, but because of the perverse incentives contained within the benefit system which makes welfare dependency too attractive.

Many lone parents, he suggests, abuse the social security system—the implication (not a new one in right wing circles) is that somehow social security systems are there to be abused; and, if we want to stop the abuse, then perhaps we had better remove the security. However, and perhaps more importantly, he argues that even without abuse the system is too generous to lone parents, especially when compared to its treatment of married couples. This is because the couple rate of Income Support is below the rate for two individuals, and because more generous earnings rules have been introduced for lone parents to help them support themselves through paid employment. Of course, the couple rate applies to non-married, as well as married couples, and this is a rule which is on occasions quite stringently enforced to the cost of lone parents and their children. No doubt Murray would claim that it is also often abused; but this is a different point more related to his general attack on all social security.

Benefit dependency and the problem of the relative treatment of couples, individuals and lone parents are well-known issues within social security policy debate. And various proposals have been made to resolve, or restructure them. Murray suggests two 'short term' measures, which in fact would probably draw support from a wide range of political and policy opinion, at least on the left; moving to full employment and removing the benefit differential between couples and single people. It is a pity he did not explore these in a little more depth, and with a little more commitment, for they both raise important issues.

But he dismisses full employment because it will not affect illegitimacy—his only concern. And he questions whether *disaggregation* (as some of the supporters of individualised benefits would call it) would be affordable in public spending terms.

More specifically, however, Murray does not just want to equalise the treatment of marriage in public policy, he wants to penalise illegitimacy. Illegitimacy was penalised economically in the past, and there was less of it then. So penalise it now, and it will decline again. To do this Murray has a disarmingly simple proposition; restore the benefit system of 1960.

Once again this demonstrates Murray's somewhat over simplistic model of social causation. If we had the benefits of 1960, then the society of 1960 would come back too. If only it would, and I could look forward to the Beatles, England winning the World Cup and the man on the moon. But it would not. History does not repeat itself. In a constantly changing world some things may appear cyclical (economic booms and recessions?), but none are repetitions. In a myriad of complex and overlapping ways social circumstances are always unique to their time. A benefit system modelled on that of 1960 might, or might not, be a policy prescription for the late 1990s, but it will not recreate 1960s values or social structures.

Actually in any case I suspect that Murray is not advocating a return to all aspects of 1960 social security policy—the insurance principle played a greater role then. His particular concern is with a means of reducing the benefits available to lone mothers in the belief that this will discourage illegitimacy—in fact not reducing them but eliminating them. Once the perverse incentives argument is accepted reduction, or removal, of benefit is the inevitable policy move, as Murray has argued before. Repeating it once again here, however, does not make it any more desirable or feasible as social policy.

It is not *desirable* because it will lead to extreme, and possibly fatal, hardship. And this hardship will not just be visited upon those whom Murray, and others, might wish morally to condemn. If all unmarried mothers, and necessarily therefore their children too, are deprived of benefits (single, separated, divorced or widowed), many good parents and deserving children, by anyone's measure, will be cruelly deprived. In a political democracy no government could realistically countenance such a move. And if an attempt were made to separate the 'deserving parents and children from the 'undeserving' (an old theme here) then practically, and legally, the drawing of lines would be fraught with insurmountable difficulties. For instance, are divorced women to be provided for and separated women not? And, if so, what about the perverse incentives introduced there?

Basing social security policy on the presumed fear of perverse incentives is also, however, not *feasible* as social policy. This would presume that individuals make decisions about the future of their life courses based only on narrow, calculated economic gains, and that therefore they could, and should, be penalised for making the wrong choices. First year sociology students soon learn that all the decisions that we make, or think we make, are structured by a range of social, cultural and economic forces within which we move but without which we cannot step. And social policy students are taught that the purpose of policy planning can only be to aim to meet broad and predictable social needs, rather to seek to shape individual circumstances actions or desires, which will inevitably vary so widely.

Of course, all social policy is, to adopt Murray's own terminology, to some extent a form of social engineering. By providing or not providing, for people's needs we may indeed shape their behaviour. But this takes place at the level of general social and economic structures rather than individual persuasion. Murray seems to eschew such social engineering; and yet by proposing to penalise lone parents by withdrawing financial support for them and their children (where this is not available elsewhere—where it is, benefit is currently withdrawn) he is in fact recommending this in its crudest, and cruellest, form. As a prescription for social policy such individual persuasion is neither feasible nor desirable; and, thankfully, therefore, the call for it is likely to fall on deaf ears.

Victorian Values

The other side of the coin to Murray's concern with the moral degeneration of the New Rabble, is his belief in the resurrection amongst the upper middle class of a sexual Puritanism and desire for matrimony which he associates, terminologically at

47

least, with a renewal of Victorian morality. This belief, he admits, is not based, as he claims his other predictions are, on statistical projections of recent social trends; but rather on the expectation that the opinion-forming generation which experienced the 'sexual revolution' of the 1960s and who are now in their late forties are going to be converted to religion and fidelity as their life course progresses, and are going to pass such values on to their children—who will follow these because they are true.

I shall return shortly to Murray's 'truths'. But I must admit first some surprise at the powerful role he seems to assign to the 'flower power generation'—'their remarkable power to define the *zeitgeist*' (his italics). No reason is advanced to explain why this generation, as opposed to any other before or after it, should have such a remarkable power. One might accept an assertion that all generations achieve such power as they reach their fifties, and thus begin to occupy most of the influential positions in government, commerce and media. But then the influence of this generation, for good or ill, would be like any other a passing phase.

As one of this cohort myself, I might be flattered to believe that we had achieved what no-one before us could, some major shift in the balance of ideological influence across the generations. But I do not. It is preposterous and self-deluding to presume that the values of any one generation can transcend, or subvert, those of others. Some people in their fifties may, as their life course develops, convert to religion or change their views on relationships; but I cannot see why this should have any more influence in the next decade than it has had in any other. Murray is confusing cohort changes with cultural changes here. Nor can I see why it is a phenomenon which will be restricted to the upper middle class, as Murray suggests. Life course changes affect all social classes. Of course in other classes other influences will be different, and perhaps Murray's perverse incentives allegations are re-entering here. But the perverse incentives would in any case apply only to those on benefits—too many people, no doubt; but not everybody outside the upper middle class.

Even if some middle class people in their fifties do become more puritanical over the next decade, therefore, I cannot see how the argument that this will have (counter)-revolutionary social consequences can be sustained sociologically. Nor can I see how, or why, this could be championed as a return to Victorian values.

Amongst the upper middle class, Victorian family life in Britain was hierarchical and formal, rather than warm and caring; parenting was carried out largely by servants and school-masters (and mistresses); prostitution, pornography and sexual double standards were rife. Amongst the working class family life was conducted against a background of grinding poverty in which early child death took a heavy toll of both children and their mothers; older children were forced into early and unrewarding employment; and marriage rates were low by modern standards. Going back to 1960, as I have suggested, is not on—but it might have been seen as a desirable trip. Going back to the future in Victorian England would make the kind of horror story better referred to Stephen Spielberg than to John Major. Perhaps Victorian America (if that is an appropriate term) was different; but somehow I doubt it.

The 'True' Values

Murray is not, in fact, advocating a return to Victorian values, any more than he is advocating equal treatment for couples and individuals in social security, or the implementation of full employment, or more generous provision for the frail elderly. These are all tangential arguments to the main thrust of his now much clearer call to arms. Murray wants to champion marriage (presumably lifelong marriage, although he does not specify this) and to condemn illegitimacy. He calls these 'traditional' values and 'free institutions'; and he claims that they are desirable because they are 'true'.

Particularly towards the end of this most recent work on the 'British Revolution' Murray's support for traditional marriage sounds more like the preaching of a revivalist church minister than the analysis and policy prescription of an academic social scientist. To assert the truth of your own values, and conse-quently to dismiss all others, is a curious form of social debate. It is tactically strong, but strategically weak. Of course all who agree with you will be forced to adopt the prescriptions which you then evolve, even though they may have misgivings about some of their practical effects. But all those who do not agree can readily ignore the prescriptions by rejecting the premises; and where the prescriptions are likely to cause significant pain there is little other cause for them to give your proposals any credence.

In short Murray is asserting that it is true that marriage is always better than cohabitation or lone parenthood as a family form, and therefore it is justifiable to punish the latter forms in order to encourage the former. The evidence which he adduces in the early part of the paper does not entirely prove this assertion; but that does not matter if it is true anyway—support for marriage is an act of faith. But, if it is an act of faith, then why bother with the evidence at all? If the concern is with moral prescription, why bother with social science?

Another Agenda

In the single-minded pursuit of the devil of illegitimacy, Murray has departed in 1994 from some of the other aspects of the, alleged, problem of the emerging underclass identified in 1989, notably unemployment and criminality. And in his concern to advocate only the penalisation of unmarried mothers, he skirts over other policy recommendations concerning employment and support for couples and individuals. These are clearly no longer his primary concerns; but they are very much the concerns of others, including, I suspect, some of those who invited him back over to Britain five years on.

In the last five years Britain has experienced a major economic recession. The Prime Minister was forced to resign, by her own party. Economic policy has been subject to a series of disastrous U-turns, once within one day! Major changes in social policy in social security, health, education and social services have come into effect. Inequalities have continued to grow; and, despite government promises, taxes have been increased.

In Britain, and perhaps more interestingly in Western Europe more generally, concern has continued to develop about growing levels of poverty. These are now widely referred to as the problem of *social exclusion*—a less pejorative term than the underclass or Murray's New Rabble, although no doubt he would say 'the more's the pity'. Encapsulated in the term social exclusion is the problem of the interplay between the social and economic forces which are marginalising large groups of people who are more or less permanently outside of the labour force (including, but hardly exclusively, many lone parents) and the experience of this process by those who are the primary victims of it. It is a problem of class polarisation, of economic inactivity and disappearing opportunities, of demographic and cultural upheaval, and of the pressure to adapt social policy to meet the rapidly changing circumstances of people whose past expectations, and hopes, no longer meet their current needs.

The high levels of economic inactivity therefore require us to re-address what we mean by full employment, and how we might move forward in generating appropriate work. The growing crime rates, and even faster growing fear of them, are forcing us to debate how we might prioritise policing to best effect, how we might aim to prevent crime, and how we could better support its victims. Demographic change is requiring that we reconsider our provision for care of the elderly and infirm, and also that we ensure that children receive support where their parents are unable to provide adequately for them.

It is in this latter area that one of the most interesting of policy innovations affecting lone parents has been introduced in Britain during this period: the Child Support Agency. Given the commitment that this represents to seek to ensure that the obligations of fathers towards their children (legitimate or illegitimate) at least at a financial level are met wherever possible, it is surprising that Murray makes no comment on it. Controversy certainly surrounds some aspects of the Agency's mission and its practice; but it is, potentially at least, a serious, and practical, attempt to enforce familial obligations, and to protect children; and there are few who object to the basic principles behind it. As a means of ensuring an improved future for the children of lone parents it is certainly a better starting point than the withdrawal of all social protection advocated by Murray, but perhaps it comes too close to condoning rather than condemnation to fit with the puritanical zeal of his new moral crusade.

As I said at the beginning, it is what Murray is not saying, rather than what he is saying, that is most significant about these comments he makes on his brief return to examine social change in Britain. He seems to have moved away from the centre stage debate about socio-economic change and social dislocation to concentrate only on a side-show performance where he preaches about the true morality of matrimony. He thus has little, or nothing, to say about the major policy developments and future policy priorities which face commentators and politicians in this country; and his prescriptions for action, directed at the false devil of illegitimacy, will I fear meet neither the challenge of practical politics nor the rigours of academic debate.

Notes

1   Charles Murray, *The Emerging British Underclass*, London: IEA Health and Welfare Unit, 1990, p. 68.
2   Brown, J.C., in *The Emerging British Underclass*, 1990.

Fundamentally Flawed

Miriam David

Charles Murray, as ever, writes in a fluent and intuitively readable but provocative style. However, also as ever, his arguments are fundamentally flawed in numerous respects. He lacks an appreciation, first, of the characteristics of British society, its social class structure and social and policy processes and tries to present arguments based upon the United States as if they automatically applied to Britain, without careful reconsideration. Secondly, and perhaps far more importantly, he lacks understanding of the methods of the social sciences and in particular the uses of social and economic statistics. Thus his arguments about the characteristics and consequences of the growth in the underclass are completely fallacious and misrepresented in this paper, leading to a gross form of caricature or stereotyping. In this reply I hope to demonstrate the ways in which these stereotypes have been erroneously developed through this kind of unscientific argument. Moreover, his arguments are predicated on moral rather than scientific reasoning and his politics appear to be obscured in simplistic but apparently appealing, to quote him, 'horribly sexist' sets of claims. He admits as much both at the end as well as the beginning of his essay by commenting on the changed 'public mood'.

Charles Murray argues that over the five year period since he was last in Britain there has been both an acceptance of his argument about the underclass in the public arena and a continuing growth in the underclass which indeed, according to him, substantiates his view. He does not, however, define what he means by the underclass but instead uses three 'criteria' to present his case, although this time the focus is mainly on the second and third of these. These are the growth in what he calls 'violent crime', secondly the growth in the rate of illegitimacy and thirdly in economic inactivity among what he chooses to call 'working aged men' (not, I hope, meaning elderly men in employment). He elaborates his arguments about these three trends but particularly those of births out-of-wedlock and developments in the family more generally linked to changes in unemployment. He then draws a number of policy conclusions.

In none of his arguments does he try to address the age specific characteristics of these three trends; but attempts instead to make correlations between the gross figures of crime, illegitimacy and unemployment as if they could be seen as having causal relationships. In other words, his general argument is that these three factors together make up the underclass and because there has been a general upward trend in each, which he shows for illegitimacy and unemployment on an area or local authority basis, this means that the argument is 'proved'. But this is to commit the Durkheimian error of correlating gross social trends with each other to prove something that might not have any kind of causal relationship. Durkheim's arguments about suicide, whilst intuitively reasonable and interesting, have on many occasions been shown to be fallacious. We simply have no evidence from the data that Murray presents as to whether or not there is a causal relationship between illegitimacy and unemployment or violent crime for that matter. Indeed it is as reasonable to argue that unemployment amongst men of working age is highest amongst the over fifties (so perhaps that is why Murray refers to them as 'working aged men') as it is to argue that illegitimacy only occurs amongst the young and teenagers, say the 15 to 24 year-olds. And although we do know that men tend to have relationships with younger women (and indeed amongst married couples two thirds of men are older than their wives) it is unlikely that the majority of these men skip a generation in choosing their partners for sexual relationships and/or procreation.

More importantly, the cornerstone of Murray's argument about the underclass is the rapid growth in illegitimacy such that, by the early 1990s, a third of all children in England and Wales are now born out-of-wedlock. This is indeed a dramatic, and perhaps staggering, figure and it certainly is worthy of consideration and explanation. However, given the fact that *one third* of births are now illegitimate, the explanation surely cannot simply be that of the underclass. Indeed if the trend continues, as Murray himself asserts that it will, it could be seen to be the *over- or majority-class* in the not too distant future. Moreover, the characteristics of this group cannot necessarily be seen as homogeneous. Again, Murray assumes that all mothers of illegitimate children are inevitably poor and/or working class and young, even teenage. Indeed he sets out yet again on his spurious mission to 'prove' this thesis.

He begins his argument on the premise that there have been *'revolutionary'* trends in the family and that the changes are new and require a new interpretation. I have absolutely no quarrel with this argument, only over the specifics of how he spells it out and the perverse policy conclusions which he ultimately draws. First his 'new interpretation' is that the changes in the family have led to a 'deterioration only in the lower class ... the upper middle class is in better shape than most people think, and it is likely to get better' (p. 5). He gets to this assertion by rather dubious and indeed circuitous means covering illegitimacy, divorce, cohabitation and social class. He starts off by delving far back into history and using ecclesiastical records to demonstrate the trends in illegitimacy. However, it is extremely difficult to compare ecclesiastical data with census or other social statistics data collected by 'modern' means. And indeed, social and family historians are forever quarrelling about the meanings and significance to be attached to such different forms of evidence. Even if Murray's argument is only intended to be journalistic rather than real scholarship, it is simply sloppy not to acknowledge the difficulties in these kinds of comparison and interpretation.

His second set of arguments about the changes in the family relates to trends in divorce and cohabitation. Again he asserts that the growing trend towards divorce 'proves' that marriage is now less meaningful than it used to be. This is indeed a curious interpretation of the nature of 'meaningfulness'. In fact, sociologists and family historians across the social and political spectrum have drawn a variety of conclusions about these trends. For example, one of the most famous in Britain, Ronald Fletcher, argues that the trends in divorce and remarriage demonstrate the continuing popularity of marriage as an institution and indeed he also shows how the rates of marriage and remarriage have never been higher.[1] Similarly but from a completely different perspective, Delphy and Leonard argue that, despite the changing rates of divorce, marriage remains a key institution of family life in capitalism, drawing their examples from both Britain and France today.[2]

Murray also uses flimsy evidence about cohabitation to assert that marriage is now less 'meaningful'. He admits that the trends in cohabitation, however, also show that three-quarters of all illegitimate births are registered in the names of both parents who are also living at the same address. This leads him to the 'conclusion' that 70 per cent of children live with married couples, 16 per cent with unmarried couples and 14 per cent with women living alone. He also links the trends in cohabitation to social policy and erroneously assumes that all such families, in other words lone mother families, are in receipt of social welfare benefits. He does not seem to be aware that the cohabitation rule is alive and well in Britain in the 1990s just as it was in the 1970s, even though its form may have altered to be slightly less draconian in terms of snoopers!

The supposed strength of Murray's case about the revolutionary trends in the family lies in his arguments about modernity and social class and his attempt to add flesh to this by analysing small area statistics comparing trends in unemployment and illegitimacy. He focuses upon 10 'rich' or upper middle class and 10 lower working class or 'poor' areas. He then pinpoints two contrasting local authorities for detailed analysis, namely Middlesbrough as an example of a 'lower working class' community versus Wokingham as an 'upper middle class' community. He sees Wokingham as an example of a community of what he describes as 'new Victorians' and Middlesbrough as an example of a community which he chooses to depict as the 'New Rabble'. The former is one of the two-parent family type 'in good shape' whereas the latter is a prime example of a community using an entirely different 'social template' and full of illegitimate children living alone with their mothers. I must say that I personally am relieved to find that I do not live in either of these two communities with such pejorative depictions and which bear so little resemblance to the social scientific literature about communities in Britain today.

Having sketched in these two contrasting communities Murray extrapolates to the 'individual' case and asserts that this will produce a dramatically changed class structure, bifurcated into the upper middle class and lower working class each characterised by their family structure such that the two-parent family is the essence for the upper middle class and illegitimacy that for the lower working class. Whilst it would be difficult to quarrel with the view that in the late twentieth century in Britain, as in other advanced industrial societies, there are dramatic changes occurring to the class structure it is unlikely to be as simplistic as Murray would like to paint it and have us believe. And his characterisation of the upper middle class as the New Victorians is rather far-fetched as is the attribution of the lone parent families as part of, or even all of, the 'New Rabble'. Both are deeply insulting to the members of these social groups whether they are new or not.

Even more of an insulting caricature is the example he draws of members of the 'New Rabble' claiming social benefits. He present us with the fictitious character of Scully who is quite simply a 'rogue extraordinaire', falsely claiming housing and other social benefits etc. Oddly the character is a *male* and it is not at all clear who his partner is and whether or not he cohabits. Presumably the example is meant to show an unemployed man, scrounging off both his lone parent partner and the welfare state and, by implication, compelled to do so by having grown up in a lone mother household with no father role model on which to rely! All this leads Murray to his overly dramatised critique of the British system of income maintenance and social welfare. He does, however, seem to feel that in this respect the chief problem is unemployment not illegitimacy.

In his confusion, therefore, he presents us with both a critique of current systems of welfare and social security and of the two main political parties. For example, he even suggests difficulties for the Labour Party as the party of the lower working class and therefore single parents or all those with illegitimate children and the Tories as that of the Wokinghams of this world. In other words, the Tories only represent the two-parent families 'who are in good shape'. This is hardly consonant with the antics of some Tory MPs to whom he even alludes.

Nevertheless, his conclusions, although muddled, are strong and morally self-righteous. He adopts the Labour Party plea for stronger policies on employment but on the grounds that if men had jobs they would be able to support their wives and children. Hence his other proposal is that women be 'persuaded' only to have children in a proper marital situation where they can be supported by their husbands (and so not go out to work, I presume!). This idea that men need families to civilise them and to 'force' them to do their patriarchal duty is ages old. A decade ago, a compatriot of Murray's, George Gilder, suggested that 'men had been cuckolded by the compassionate state' and he too recommended a social policy, to the Reagan administration, that would also aim to discourage women from having children out-of-wedlock.[3] In the 1930s in England similar social policies were also proposed although perhaps in more muted and less sexist language. These policies have been tried and tested and found wanting. It simply will not do to keep harping on about the past and the 'Golden Age' of the family. Was it really ever thus? And even if it were, why has it changed? Is it simply because women are perverse or is it because men do need to think more clearly and carefully about what they want and what is in fact possible for men and women alone and together in late twentieth century Britain or the USA? Such questions are social and cannot be answered by the sort of commentary, rather than analysis, that Murray provides.

Notes

1   Fletcher, R., *The Shaking of the Foundations: Family and Society*, London: Routledge, 1988.
2   Delphy, C. and Leonard, D., *Familiar Exploitation*, Cambridge: Polity Press, 1992.
3   Gilder, G., *Wealth and Poverty*, New York: Basic Books, 1981.

Where Are the New Victorians?

Melanie Phillips

Charles Murray is like a bit of chewing gum that gets stuck to the sole of your shoe. You scrape it off in disgust, but your shoe still sticks to the pavement as you walk. When you remove the shoe and peel off the remainder of the offending gum, you find the sole comes away in your hands. It was rotten anyway. It was all too vulnerable to attack.

It is impossible to shake off Murray's analysis of Britain's underclass because it has exposed a decay at the core of our society that most of us would prefer to ignore. Reactions to Murray, among those who are politically of the centre or of the left, are violent and troubled. There are those who dismiss him as unspeakably vile, for whom his name will never pass their lips except as an expletive, who denounce the very word 'underclass' as an anathema never to be used in civilised society. For them, the situation of our poorest communities, their lifestyle, behaviour and attitudes are largely to be accepted without adverse comment. And where some blame is clearly called for, any such criticism must be laid squarely at the door of the government for reducing these communities to this plight.

But there are others of whom I am one, no less opposed to Conservative politics, who are fascinated and repelled by Murray's analysis in almost equal measure. For us, he has drawn attention to an alarming social development which cannot wholly be explained away as the outcome of economic circumstances. We recognise that this is a cultural phenomenon which owes as much to egalitarian social individualism as to the brutalities of the free market. But at the same time we recoil from the selective nature of his analysis, not to mention his scorched earth solution.

Like Murray, I believe that the progressive collapse of the intact family is bringing about a set of social changes which is taking us into uncharted and terrifying waters. Like Murray, I recognise that there are now whole communities, framed by structural unemployment, in which fatherlessness has become the norm. These communities are truly alarming because children are being brought up with dysfunctional and often antisocial attitudes as a direct result of the fragmentation and emotional chaos of households in which sexual libertarianism provides a stream of transient and unattached men servicing their mothers. But unlike Murray, I do not believe that the collapse of the intact family is confined to the lower social classes. I do not believe that it has been caused by the welfare state. And I most certainly do not believe that the solution is effectively to starve poor women and children back into marriage.

The collapse of the family may take different forms in different social classes, but its roots and its effects are the same. Fragmented families cause children hardship and disadvantage. Relatively speaking, children whose families are no longer intact do worse in virtually every area of life than children from intact families, looked after throughout their childhood by their own father and mother. That holds true for middle-class children as much as for children from lower social classes. Children's problems are by no means confined to those brought up by single parents. Step-parents often create worse problems. The distress and damage done to a middle-class child shunted around between step-households may take the form of depression, eating disorders, educational under-achievement and an inability to form lasting adult relationships; they are no less destructive than the effects on the lower-class child who may truant, sniff glue and drift into crime.

The accelerating rates of divorce, cohabitation and out-of-wedlock births are being driven along by the revolution in women's expectations and economic circumstances. And while it is obviously the case, as Murray suggests, that middle-class women have been economically liberated through employment while women at the bottom of the pile have been economically freed by welfare benefits, it is perverse to target attention and blame on those lower-class women. Our whole culture has devalued marriage to a breakable contract of little intrinsic worth, and children to merely another set of consumer commodities. We have created a society in which children are increasingly expected to satisfy adult rights to individual fulfilment, rather than be the repository of adult duties and responsibilities.

Advances in embryology are underscoring this new and

amoral attitude towards children. Their best interests are being discarded along a line of family dismemberment which leads all the way from virgin births to serial partners. From self-impregnation courtesy of the local sperm bank to multiple monogamy, fathers are increasingly participating in the family, in A.H. Halsey's pungent phrase, as no more than a genital. Popular culture overwhelmingly proclaims these messages. As I write, current issues of women's magazines promise: 'Why men walk out; three men who left their partner' and 'My wife and mistress are both pregnant', *Marie-Claire*; 'Sex and the single girl; when he decides it's over', *Cosmopolitan*; 'When sex is brilliant but the relationship stinks', *19*. Every day, every week, every month, magazines, films, TV, popular music, tabloid and so-called quality newspapers, all conform to the same cultural expectations.

Clearly, it is not welfare that's created these new social norms. Yet Murray not only draws on statistical evidence to support such an analysis, but goes even further to suggest that while the lower orders are all breeding like illegitimate rabbits, the middle classes are rediscovering marriage, fidelity and responsibility. Hence his division of British society into the New Victorians and the New Rabble. This is not merely viciously offensive but it is bunk. Murray's trick is to put sets of statistics side by side and then extrapolate from them theories of cause and effect. Not surprisingly, they don't stand up to scrutiny. The situation is much more complex. As he himself concedes, his prediction of New Victorianism is just that, 'pure prediction, not an extrapolation from existing trends'. He adduces not a shred of evidence to support this prediction; not surprisingly, because the trends are going in the opposite direction.

According to the OPCS *Birth Statistics 1992*, since the beginning of the 1980s jointly registered births outside marriage increased three to four fold for *each* social class. And the greatest increase was in Classes I and II. So much for the New Victorians. Murray makes much of the fact that more illegitimate babies are being born to the lower social classes. But again the facts are more complex. The lower classes have more babies. According to the 1991 Census, there were 1,756,093 people in Social Classes IV and V and the skilled manual class, compared to 1,849,893 people in Classes I and II and the skilled non-manual class. But although there were nearly 100,000 fewer of them, the lower social group gave birth to more babies: 336,000 compared to 258,000. According to these figures, Social Classes IV and V produce more babies proportionate to their numbers than Classes I and II. Moreover, so far from being a rabble it is the skilled working class that produces the most jointly registered births outside marriage. And it is that very same social class that turns out to be producing the most children *inside* marriage as well.

Murray's statistics, therefore, are selective and misleading. They are selected to back up his theory that lower working class illegitimacy is the problem. The question has to be asked why he concentrates so heavily on this selective interpretation at the expense of a more comprehensive and accurate, if more complex, analysis. It is hard to ignore the fact that Murray himself is divorced and has fathered children in two households. What appears to be acceptable behaviour for himself, a middle-class man who can afford to maintain such a lifestyle, is to be condemned among those who are less well-heeled. Maybe therefore it's not surprising that divorce hardly figures in Murray's social apocalypse. Yet all the evidence suggests that for many children it is the end of their world.

The collapse of the intact family is a social disaster. It weakens the cultural and moral transmitters down through the generations. It lies at the heart of many of our social problems. Personally, I believe that if we are unable to check it we will produce a society dangerously divided not along social class lines, as Murray suggests, but *within* each class. The barricades will go up between intact families whose members prosper and who can form constructive civic bonds and fractured families whose members are desperately disadvantaged and who cannot connect and form constructive communities.

We may not be able to do anything about this. Maybe, as many suggest, these new social patterns are irreversible. But if we are going to have any chance of halting our slide over the social precipice, we're not going to achieve it by treating part of our society as alien, a race apart, a rabble. We are one society. These cultural developments run through it as a fault line from top to bottom. So any remedy has to be comprehensive and fair, not divisive and vindictive. If the plant is once again to bloom, it is the roots that have to be treated. We shouldn't just chop off some of the leaves.

I believe that there are serious limits to what the state can do to change people's behaviour. People will only change the way in which they live if they are convinced that it is in their interests and the interests of their society for them to do so, and that the social consequences of not doing so are too severe to be tolerated. Intellectuals and politicians therefore bear an enormous responsibility to stop peddling the silly lie that the dismembered family is no worse than the intact family. And the middle classes bear a heavy responsibility too to re-affirm *by their own behaviour* the desirability of bringing up children inside a stable marriage. How the middle classes behave has huge resonance for classes lower down the social scale, since it is the middle classes to which they aspire and whose lifestyle they wish to share.

But however limited the role of the state may be, it does play some part in this process. At present, for example, the tax and benefits systems produce some perverse anti-marriage effects. These should be reversed, not merely because economic circumstances play *some* part in determining people's lifestyles but because law and public policy have a significant declaratory effect which should not be under-estimated. They help announce the moral standards a society thinks are desirable. The dilemma, however, is producing a political and economic culture that actively favours marriage which does not in its train punish the children in dismembered families and make their predicament even worse than it already is.

Our society does not at present publicly declare itself in favour of marriage; quite the opposite. We must do so, while finding a way through the dilemma to protect *all* children. This means not cutting off all welfare benefits to single mothers, but offering more carrot than stick to make marriage the attractive option. At the same time, the declaratory route should mean that divorce should not be made easier and assisted fertility should only be provided for married couples. It is probably the middle classes who would scream loudest at such unequivocal support for marriage. That is the measure of the problem we face. It is also the measure of the vindictive irrelevance of any solution that merely targets the poor.

Would You Take One Home With You?

Sue Slipman

Our century has plotted its course through the growth of individual rights. This process accelerated in the 1960s and when, in the 1980s, the libertarian free marketeers broke the post war consensus, they broke up our traditional social framework of inter-locking obligations. All these changes happened within a period of massive economic, industrial and technological change. The 1990s have given rise to the growth of a breed of moral panickers who are alarmed at the changes wrought within the social fabric and in particular within the institution of the family and who now wish to re-assert a new agenda that is based on duties not rights. The problem they face is that the last twenty years and more have taken society's lid off the box. The force required to shove it firmly back on requires a methodology that it is totally out of sync with our secular, pluralist humanitarian democracy.

I do not wish to be entirely churlish to the alarmists. There are some grounds for agreement. We clearly need to take stock of social change and recognise that the combination of factors causing change risk creating a social order in which greed and easy self-fulfilment become the norm. I agree with Charles Murray that there are new values in gestation and that some of them will be welcome. They include trustworthiness, and meeting the duties that responsibility for others confers upon you. But we will not, I hope, move back to an outmoded hypocrisy that denies human freedom and growth.

Unlike the panickers I do not believe that all the changes over these twenty years have been deleterious. Some changes have brought positive good and have developed a story that has taken as long as the century to unfold. I am hopeful that we can incorporate the positive changes over these years whilst we address their downside. We could move on to a new order in which rights and duties balance each other and in which human freedoms will be exercised alongside human responsibilities.

The Victorian family that now delights Murray and others hid the powerlessness of women and children as property within the family. It is true that the family as male property has been the traditional method of socialising and containing the warrior in man, but the twentieth century has been a battle for women and children to have rights of their own within the structure of the family in a way that has encroached upon the power of men. They can now in theory negotiate with men, but the family has become an arena of conflict in which individuals fight for enough space, power and share in the resources they need to sustain them.

The moral panickers demonise the one-parent family but it is more accurately and properly understood as a result of the modern conflict within the two-parent family, coupled with the process of sharp industrial and economic change. Lone parenthood is the result of major societal changes—not their cause.

Lone parents are not a breed apart. They hold the same moral values as everyone else. They want the same access to success for their children and they are as prepared as all other parents to take responsibility for them. Indeed if they did not do so on a day-to-day basis our social problems would be a lot more pressing than they are. Moreover most lone parents would give their eye teeth for a decent relationship with a partner to support them in parenting. Few chose to be lone parents.

Murray's analysis concentrates on the rate of births outside marriage. But the majority of lone parents on benefit are mature men and women who have been married. He also dismisses the dramatic rise in cohabitation as having no real significance in mitigating the numbers. The truth is that we do not know how many never married lone parents have been cohabiting—but the indications are that a fair number believed they were in a stable partnership.

Murray takes the period of Victorian industrialisation and argues that if rapid change and modernity were the cause of lone parenthood it would have been seen in this era, but in fact the rate of non-marital children declined. What he fails to take into account is that the rise of the factory and manufacturing industries created large numbers of jobs that paid for marriages and sustained families. The technological era is vastly different. The industrial revolution ushered in the age of trade union aspirations for the family wage. We now live in an age when income from wages for many families needs supplementing from the benefit system. Part-time jobs in McDonalds cannot provide like full-time manufacturing jobs.

Certainly the unskilled manual working class are producing less stable unions between men and women. It is here that the traditional nuclear family is under most pressure. In the nuclear family men were the breadwinners and women the childrearers. The death of the staple industries killed off the family form and the communities that were once sustained by the family wage earned by the male. There are no more mothers than there have ever been in these communities; there are just fewer committed fathers.

Men in Social Class V are unlikely ever again to be breadwinners. Murray argues that full employment is part of the solution, but he acknowledges that this will not by itself ensure that women will be prepared to marry men. But even if a return to full-employment on the traditional model is the desirable solution—it is not going to happen. The new jobs coming on stream are better suited to the working patterns and skills of women rather than men. This has produced a challenge to male identity. The traditional routes for men into adulthood of wage earning and authority figure in the family are no longer open. They have lost their traditional role but they have not found another one that would make them attractive to women. The resulting conflict between men and women has lead to an increase in domestic violence over these years of change: a phenomenon that Murray dismisses as insignificant. Our police thankfully take it more seriously.

Accompanying changes to the industrial structure has been the rise of female ambition. Most women now work. They are less willing to accept a subservient role within the family than they once did when dependent upon male industry for an income. But most women still want to have children and, from what we can tell, most still aspire to a decent relationship with a partner as the best way of bringing up those children. Very few women chose lone parenthood. Most of those who do are middle class, professional women who can usually afford the costs of their child. If there is a new model for relationships between men and women it will be based on partnership where both partners have to work towards acquiring family income —and in many cases they will need ongoing subsidy from the state to tackle in-work poverty.

Men and women in higher social classes are more likely to achieve positive partnerships as parents. They have far more affluence to lose in breaking their relationships than do those lower down the social scale. Dual earner couples enjoy very affluent life styles. Domestic responsibilities continue to fall more heavily upon women regardless of their work patterns. But, high income couples can pay someone else to do their cleaning and look after their children, allowing both partners enough freedom. They do not have to confront the conflict between their freedom as individuals and being left holding the baby.

As you move down the social class structure these pressures upon the combining of roles of parent and worker become more obvious. In Social Class V both roles now fall more heavily upon women, men having largely absented themselves from the process. Increasingly if men have little to bring to the family party and women continue to sustain the burden of parenting and breadwinning—they will go on questioning what is the point of a man.

Murray argues that rising crime is directly connected to all these facets. It stands to reason that it is infinitely harder to bring up a child alone and to provide resources than it is to do so with a committed partner. Indeed most lone parents live on the poverty line with few resources. You would expect to find a higher incidence of delinquent activity from children in one- than two-parent families, and you do. It is nine per cent for two-parent families and 16 per cent for one-parent families. But most of this crime is petty juvenile misbehaviour—not serious crime—and more importantly you cannot base a public policy on the fact that 84 per cent of lone parents are doing a good job in bringing up their children.

It is true that what is happening to our young men is very worrying. It appears that as the traditional routes into adulthood no longer exist for them, many have removed themselves from any concept of parental responsibility. Increasingly when the sex that they see as purely recreational becomes procreation they react as if they had no role in the process. I would be a rich woman if I had a pound for every time I have heard a man talk about 'these girls who make themselves pregnant'.

I have no doubt that removal of men from parenting is extremely bad for their development as civilised human beings. They are being infantilised and there is a crisis in male identity. But any discussion about the family which is gender neutral will inevitably get it wrong. Furthermore any discussion about the family which does not call for men to change or for wealth and power to be more fairly distributed between family members, necessarily wishes to return traditional power and authority to men.

So, it comes as no surprise that Murray's radical solutions are to punish women and children back into dependence upon men. He would starve them back into such dependence. But if men cannot meet that dependence through work there is no point in doing this apart from trying to make the working class behave more like the middle class, to curb the power of uppity women and to stop the lower orders from breeding excessively. Eugenicists have been trying to do that from time immemorial.

Murray is right that the benefit system allows women and children to survive without men, but it is not the cause of the breakdown in relations between men and women. It is not only more humane, it also makes better sense to assist lone parents to economic independence, whilst we find better strategies to socialise men to accept power sharing and responsibility with women.

I have no doubt that such a strategy involves a new consensus around parental responsibility based on an acceptance that the child has rights and parents have duties regardless of their marital relationship. This consensus has to be shored up by a successful operation on the part of the Child Support Agency ensuring that all parents at least fulfil the basic duty of maintaining their child.

The values of parental responsibility have to be taught in our schools alongside sex education and a new emotional literacy amongst young men. We need a positive programme to prevent teenage parenthood by enhancing the self esteem of the young to make them less likely to succumb to peer group pressure for early sexual activity for which they may not be emotionally equipped. Ensuring that girls leave school with qualifications and job prospects would be recognition that all too many will be left holding the baby.

We will also need programmes of support to enable young parents to be competent parents. Helping all lone parents to work so that they build their self esteem and give their children a stable working pattern to aspire to as well as cutting costs to the tax payer may be crucial. But forcing them to work full time so that they cannot supervise their adolescent children may be a disaster.

Cutting state benefits for mothers will make our problems worse, not better. The divorced or separated mother is in exactly the same financial position as the never married mother under our system. Charles Murray's prescription will simply ensure that, regardless of their route into lone parenthood, mothers and children will not survive. He openly admits that he has a misogynist agenda ('It is all horribly sexist I know') but he still cannot explain why any woman in her right mind should want to take one of his new rabble home with her.

Also Half-Price

The Family: Is It Just Another Lifestyle Choice?, Jon Davies (Editor), Brigitte Berger and Allan Carlson £6.95, 120pp, 1993, ISBN: 0-255 36276-5

Three essays examine the consequences for individuals and for society of the breakdown of the traditional family. They argue that the family is not just another 'lifestyle choice', but vital to Western civilisation.

"The report says that society is paying a heavy price for the belief that the family is just another lifestyle choice." *The Times*

Equal Opportunities: A Feminist Fallacy, Caroline Quest (Editor), *et al.* £6.95, 111pp, June 1992, ISBN: 0-255 36272 2

"Laws banning sex discrimination and promoting equal pay at work damage the interests of women the Institute of Economic Affairs claims today."
The Daily Telegraph

"Let us not above all be politically correct. Let us not become overheated because the Institute of Economic Affairs has brought out a startling report entitled *Equal Opportunities: A Feminist Fallacy.*"
The Times

Citizenship and Rights in Thatcher's Britain: Two Views, Norman Barry and Raymond Plant £3.95, 77pp, June 1990, ISBN: 0-255 36261-7

Two leading political theorists describe and discuss the rights and obligations of citizenship, Professor Plant arguing from a socialist standpoint and Professor Barry from a classical-liberal perspective.

Christian Capitalism or Christian Socialism?, Michael Novak, Professor Ronald Preston, £4.95, 40pp, April 1994, ISBN: 0-255 36352-4

"*Christian capitalism or Christian socialism?* The latter question alone will send mitres tumbling from episcopal heads in outrage ... *Capitalism*—the creed of Victorian mill-owners and Wall Street plutocrats? How can capitalism be, well, Christian?"
Sunday Telegraph

Liberating Women ... From Modern Feminism, Caroline Quest (Ed), Norman Barry, Mary Kenny, Patricia Morgan, Joan Kennedy Taylor, Glenn Wilson £6.95, 101pp, 1994, ISBN 0-255 36353-2

Caroline Quest argues that 'power feminism' ends up having as little relevance to most women as the 'victim feminism' it is directed against. It is, she says, 'for pre-maternal young women' and 'is of little relevance and help to the realities of life for the majority of real women'.

"It would be a mistake ... to take anything but seriously the essay "Double income, no kids: the case for a family wage" by the sociologist Patricia Morgan."

Margot Norman, *The Times*

The Moral Foundations of Market Institutions, John Gray, with Chandran Kukathas, Patrick Minford and Raymond Plant, £7.95, 142pp, Feb 1992, ISBN: 0-255 36271-4

Distinguished Oxford philosopher, John Gray, examines the moral legitimacy of the market economy. While upholding the value of the market economy he insists on the importance of an 'enabling' welfare state.

"one of the most intelligent and sophisticated contributions to modern conservative philosophy."
The Times

"This powerful tract ... maps out a plausible middle ground for political debate."
Financial Times

A Moral Basis For Liberty, Father Robert Sirico, commentaries by Lord Lawson of Blaby, William Oddie £4.95, 38pp, July 1994, ISBN: 0-255 36354-0

Father Robert Sirico, a Roman Catholic priest and President of the Acton Institute defends the morality of liberty. His argument is criticised by former Chancellor of the Exchequer, Nigel Lawson, and William Oddie a regular columnist for *The Sunday Times*.

ORDER FORM—EVERYTHING HALF-PRICE

Title	Normal Price	Offer Price	Qty	£
Families Without Fatherhood (2nd Edition)	£7.95	£3.95		
Rising Crime and the Dismembered Family	£5.95	£2.95		
Reinventing Civil Society	£7.95	£3.95		
A Moral Basis for Liberty	£4.95	£2.45		
The Family: Just Another Lifestyle Choice?	£6.95	£3.45		
Equal Opportunities: A Feminist Fallacy	£6.95	£3.45		
Moral Foundations of Market Institutions	£7.95	£3.95		
The Emerging British Underclass	£5.95	£2.95		
Empowering the Parents	£6.95	£3.45		
Christian Capitalism or Christian Socialism?	£4.95	£2.45		
Citizenship and Rights in Thatcher's Britain	£3.95	£1.95		
Medical Care: Is It a Consumer Good?	£3.95	£1.95		
Liberating Women From Modern Feminism	£6.95	£3.45		

Please add 50p P&P per book up to a
maximum of £2.00

Subtotal:

P&P:

Total:

✓

I enclose a cheque for £...................... payable to the Institute of Economic Affairs ☐

Please debit my Mastercard/Visa/Amex/Diner's card for £.................... ☐

Number: ....

Expiry Date: ....

Name: ....

Address: ....

....

....

*Please return to **IEA Health and Welfare Unit, Institute of Economic Affairs,***
2 Lord North Street, Westminster, London SWIP 3LB

STILL IN PRINT—
MURRAY'S ORIGINAL CRITIQUE

NOW AVAILABLE FOR ONLY HALF-PRICE